THE FATHERS
OF THE CHURCH

A NEW TRANSLATION

VOLUME 76

THE FATHERS
OF THE CHURCH

A NEW TRANSLATION

ST. CYRIL
OF ALEXANDRIA
LETTERS 1–50

Translated by

JOHN I. McENERNEY
Villanova University
Villanova, Pennsylvania

THE CATHOLIC UNIVERSITY OF AMERICA PRESS
Washington, D.C.

Nihil obstat:
REVEREND MICHAEL SLUSSER, S.T.B., D. Phil.
Censor Deputatus

Imprimatur:
REV. MSGR. RAYMOND BOLAND
Vicar General for the Archdiocese of Washington

February 26, 1985
The nihil obstat and imprimatur are official declarations that a book or pamphlet is free of doctrinal or moral error. No implication is contained therein that those who have granted the nihil obstat and the imprimatur agree with the content, opinions or statements expressed.

LIBRARY OF CONGRESS CATALOGING-IN-PUBLICATION DATA
Cyril, Saint, Patriarch of Alexandria, ca. 370–444.
 St. Cyril of Alexandria : letters 1–50.

 (The Fathers of the Church ; v. 76)
 Bibliography: p.
 Includes index.
  1. Cyril, Saint, Patriarch of Alexandria, ca. 370–444.
 2. Christian saints—Egypt—Alexandria—Correspondence.
 I. McEnerney, John I., 1913–   . II. Title.
 III. Title: Saint Cyril of Alexandria. IV. Series.
 BR60.F3C917   1987   270.2'092'4 [B]   85-5692
 ISBN 0-8132-0076-8

TO MARY,
MOTHER OF GOD.

CONTENTS

ACKNOWLEDGMENTS

In presenting this translation of the correspondence of Cyril of Alexandria I wish to thank the libraries of The Catholic University of America, The University of Pennsylvania, Villanova University, the University of Virginia and the Krauth Memorial Library of the Lutheran Theological Seminary for assistance in providing or obtaining the rare books needed.

The translation of Letter 100 by R. Y. Ebied and L. R. Wickham from Syriac into English has been reprinted by the permission of the Editors of *The Journal of Theological Studies*.

The translation from Syriac into English of Letter 101 was done by Mr. Edward Mathews. The translation from Coptic into English of Letter 110 was done by Rev. David W. Johnson, S.J.

Gratitude is owed to the former editor of the Fathers of the Church Rev. Hermigild Dressler, O.F.M. for his scholarly advice and direction, and to Dr. John J. Dillon for his assistance and friendly advice. The same is due to the many typists who aided in the work and to Mrs. Mary McEnerney for her encouragement and help on the proofs.

John I. McEnerney
Villanova University
Villanova, Penna.

SELECT BIBLIOGRAPHY

TEXTS OF THE LETTERS

Bickell, Gustav. *Ausgewählte Schriften der Syrischen Kirchenväter Aphraates, Rabulas und Isaak von Ninive.* Kempten: Kösel, 1874.

Bouriant, U. *Fragments coptes relatifs au concile d'Éphèse.* Mémoires publiés par les membres de la Mission archéologique française au Caire. Vol. 8. Paris, 1892.

Ebied, R. Y. and L. R. Wickham. *A Collection of Unpublished Syriac Letters of Cyril of Alexandria.* CSCO 359. Louvain, 1975.

————. "An Unknown Letter of Cyril of Alexandria in Syriac." *The Journal of Theological Studies* n.s. 22(1971): 420–434.

Evetts, B. *History of the Patriarchs of the Coptic Church of Alexandria.* Arabic text edited, translated and annotated. PO 1. Paris: Firmin-Didot, 1907. Pp. 433–436.

Guidi, I. *Atti della R. Accademia dei Lincei.* Ser. 4, *rendiconti* 2. Roma, 1886. Pp. 545–547.

Joannou, Périclès-Pierre. *Fonti: Fascicolo IX: Discipline générale antique (IVᵉ–IXᵉ s.).* Vol. 1, pt. 2: *Les canons des Synodes Particuliers.* Vol. 2: *Les canons des Pères Grecs.* Pontificia commissione per la redazione del codice di diretto canonico orientale. Grottaferrata (Rome): Tipografia Italo-Orientale "S. Nilo," 1962–63.

Kraatz, Wilhelm. *Koptische Akten zum ephesinischen Konzil vom Jahre 431.* TU 11.2 n.s. Leipzig: Hinrichs, 1904.

Krusch, Bruno. *Studien zur christlich-mittelalterlichen Chronologie. Der 84 Jährige Ostercyclus und seine Quellen.* Leipzig: Von Veit, 1880.

Lebon, Joseph. *Scriptores Syri 46. Severi Antiocheni Liber contra impium Grammaticum. Orationis tertiae pars prior.* CSCO 94. Louvain: Durbecq, 1952.

Leipoldt, J. *Scriptores Coptici.* Series 2, vol. 4: *Sinuthii archimandritae vita et opera omnia.* CSCO 42. Paris: Poussielgue, 1908.

Migne, J. P. ed. PG 76 and 77. Paris, 1863, 1859.

Overbeck J. J. *S. Ephraemi Syri, Rabbulae Edesseni, Balaei Aliorumque opera selecta.* Oxford: At the Clarendon Press, 1865.

Pusey, P. E. *Sancti Patris Nostri Cyrilli Archiepiscopi Alexandrini in D. Joannis Evangelium. Accedunt fragmenta varia necnon tractatus ad Tiberium Diaconum duo.* Oxford: At the Clarendon Press, 1872.

Richard, M. "Deux lettres perdues de Cyrille d'Alexandrie." *Studia Patristica* 7.1 (= TU 92). Ed. F. L. Cross. Pp. 274–275. Berlin: Akademie Verlag, 1966.

Schwartz, Eduard and Straub, John et al. *Acta Conciliorum Oecumenicorum.* Berlin and Leipzig: de Gruyter, 1914–.

Schwartz, Eduard. *Codex Vaticanus gr.* 1431. *Eine antichalkedonische Sammlung aus der Zeit Kaiser Zenos. Abhandlungen der Bayerischen Akademie der Wissenschaften philosophisch-philologisch und historische Klasse.* Vol. 32. Abhandlung no. 6. Munich, 1927.

OTHER WORKS

Brown, Raymond E., Fitzmyer, Joseph and Murphy, Roland E., eds. *The Jerome Biblical Commentary.* Englewood Cliffs, New Jersey: Prentice Hall, 1968.

Cross, F. L. and Livingstone, E. A., eds. *Oxford Dictionary of the Christian Church.* 2d and revised ed. Oxford: At the Clarendon Press, 1983.

Dombart, Bernard and Kalb, Alphonsus, eds. *S. Aurelii, De Civitate Dei Libri XI–XXII.* CCL 48. Turnhout: Brepols, 1955.

Du Manoir, Hubert, S. J. *Dogme et spiritualité chez saint Cyrille d'Alexandrie.* Paris: J. Vrin, 1944.

Festugière, A. J. *Éphèse et Chalcédoine Actes des Conciles.* Paris, 1892.

Garnier, Julian, ed., *Basilii Caesareae Cappadociae archiepiscopi opera omnia quae extant.* Paris: Gaume, 1839.

Geerard, Maurice. *Clavis Patrum Graecorum.* 4 vols. to date. Turnhout: Brepols, 1974–.

Grillmeier, Aloys, S.J. *Christ in Christian Tradition.* Vol. 1: *From the Apostolic Age to Chalcedon (451).* 2d ed. Translated by John Bowden. Atlanta: John Knox Press, 1975.

Hefele, Charles, J. *A History of the Councils of the Church.* Edinburgh: Clark, 1883.

Hughes, Philip. *The Church in Crisis. A History of the General Councils 325–1870.* Garden City, N.Y.: Hanover House, 1961.

Jones, Charles, W. *Bedae Opera de Temporibus.* Cambridge, Mass.: The Medieval Academy of America, 1943.

Kelly, J. N. D. *Early Christian Doctrines.* 5th ed. London: Adam & Charles Black, 1977.

Lampe, G. W. H. *A Patristic Greek Lexicon.* Oxford: At the Clarendon Press, 1961.

Liébaert, Jacques. *La doctrine christologique de saint Cyrille d'Alexandrie avant la querelle Nestorienne.* Lille: Economat, 1951.

Lindsay, W. M., ed. *Isidori Hispalensis Etymologiae.* Oxford: At the Clarendon Press, 1911.

Loofs, Friedrich Arnim. *Nestoriana: Die Fragmente des Nestorius gesammelt, untersucht und herausgegeben.* Halle: Niemeyer, 1905.

Morris, Rudolph, et al., trans. . . .*Vincent of Lerins: Commonitories* etc. FOTC 7. Washington, D.C.: The Catholic University of America Press, 1949.

Newman, Cardinal John Henry. *Tracts.* London: Longmans, 1924.

Orchard, Bernard et al., eds. *A Catholic Commentary on Holy Scripture.* New York: Thomas Nelson & Sons, 1953.

Papadopoulos, Chrysostom. *Ho Hagios Kurillos Alexandreias.* Alexandria: Patriarchal Press, 1933.

Quasten, Johannes. *Patrology.* Reprint Westminster, Md.: Christian Classics, 1983.

Schwartz, Eduard. *Christliche und Jüdische Ostertafeln. Abhandlungen der königlichen Gesellschaft der Wissenschaften zu Göttingen.* Philosophisch-Historische Klasse 8.6 n.s. Berlin: Weidmann, 1905.

Smith, William and Wace, Henry. *A Dictionary of Christian Biography, Literature, Sects and Doctrines During the First Eight Centuries.* 4 vols. London, 1877–87.

Swete, Henry Barclay. *The Old Testament in Greek According to the Septuagint.* 3 vols. Cambridge: At the University Press, 1887–94.

Van den Dries, Joseph. *The Formula of St. Cyril of Alexandria.* Rome, 1937.

Way, Sister Agnes Clare, trans. *Saint Basil the Great: Letters Volume 2 (186–368).* FOTC 28. Washington, D.C.: The Catholic University of America Press, 1955.

Wickham, Lionel R. *Cyril of Alexandria. Select Letters.* Oxford: At the Clarendon Press, 1983.

Wiles, Maurice and Santer, Mark. *Documents in Early Christian Thought.* New York: Cambridge University Press, 1976.

Wilken, Robert L. *Judaism and the Early Christian Mind.* New Haven: Yale University Press, 1971.

Wolfson, H. A. *The Philosophy of the Church Fathers.* 3d ed. Cambridge, Mass.: Harvard University Press, 1970.

ABBREVIATIONS

SERIES PUBLICATIONS

CCL   Corpus Christianorum, Series Latina. Turnhout 1953—.

CSCO   Corpus Scriptorum Christianorum Orientalium. Louvain, 1903—.

CSEL   Corpus Scriptorum Ecclesiasticorum Latinorum. Vienna and Leipzig, 1910.

FOTC   The Fathers of the Church. New York and Washington, D.C., 1947—.

PG   Patrologiae Cursus Completus. Series Graeca. Ed. J. P. Migne. Paris, 1857–1866.

PO   Patrologia Orientalis. Ed. R. Graffin and F. Nau. Paris, 1903—.

TU   Texte und Untersuchungen zur Geschichte der Altchristlichen Literatur. Berlin, 1882—.

REFERENCE WORKS AND DICTIONARIES

ACO   *Acta Conciliorum Oecumenicorum.* Ed. E. Schwartz. Berlin 1914–.

CCHS   *A Catholic Commentary on Holy Scripture.* Ed. B. Orchard and E. Sutcliff. New York, 1953.

CPG   *Clavis Patrum Graecorum.* Ed. M. Geerard. 4 volumes. Brepols-Turnhout, 1974–83. 3 (1979).

CPL   *Clavis Patrum Latinorum.* 2d edition. Ed. E. Dekkers and E. Gaar. Steenbrugge, 1961.

JBC   *The Jerome Biblical Commentary.* Ed. R. E. Brown, J. A. Fitzmyer, R. E. Murphy. New Jersey, 1968.

LXX   *The Old Testament in Greek According to the Septuagint.* Ed. H. B. Swete. 3 vols. Cambridge, 1887–94.

ODCC²   *The Oxford Dictionary of the Christian Church.* 2d and revised ed. Ed. F. L. Cross and E. A. Livingstone. Oxford, 1983.

PGL   *A Patristic Greek Lexicon.* Ed. G. W. H. Lampe. Oxford, 1961.

Quasten   Johannes Quasten. *Patrology 3: The Golden Age of Greek Patristic Literature from the Council of Nicaea to the Council of Chalcedon.* Utrecht, 1960. Reprint. Westminster, Md., 1983.

INTRODUCTION

YRIL OF ALEXANDRIA was born during the last quarter of the fourth century and died on June 27, 444. The first certain date of his life is 403, when he was present, as he himself says in Letter 75, at the so-called Synod of the Oak near Chalcedon, at which Theophilus, Patriarch of Alexandria, deposed John Chrysostom from the See of Constantinople. After Theophilus died on October 15, 412, Cyril, his nephew, was elected and was elevated to his place as Patriarch on October 17. He ruled the See of Alexandria for thirty-two years.

(2) Most of the correspondence which has come down to us has to do with the great Christological controversy of the first half of the fifth century.[1] In the winter of 427 to 428 Nestorius, a priest of the Church of Antioch and a renowned preacher, was elevated to the See of Constantinople. In his attacks on heresy he fell into heresy himself, for he made public statements which meant that there were two persons in Christ and that the title *Theotokos*, Mother of God, could not be given to Mary. His teaching spread and reached Egypt. Some of the monks subject to Cyril's jurisdiction asked him for direction and his reply, the famous Letter 1, brought him into the forefront of the coming battle.

(3) The conflict with Nestorius resulted in him being condemned and deposed by the Council of Ephesus in 431, at

---

1. On the great Christological controversy of the first half of the fifth century, see especially A. Grillmeier, S. J., *Christ in Christian Tradition*, vol. 1: *From the Apostolic Age to Chalcedon (451)*, 2d ed., trans. J. Bowden (Atlanta, 1975), 414–483, 501–539, 543–547, 559–568; and J. N. D. Kelly, *Early Christian Doctrines*, 5th ed. (London, 1977), 130–343.

1

which Cyril presided according to the instructions of Pope
Celestine. The aftermath of the council involved Cyril in prob-
lems which cost him personally the loss of a dear friend, John
of Antioch, the disgrace of being imprisoned, the expense of
journeys and ransom, and acrimony which took several years
to eradicate. It gave him, however, an occasion to bring into
play the great mind with which he had been gifted on a topic of
vital interest and importance to the Christian world, and he
prevailed.

(4) When the Council of Ephesus met on June 22, 431, John,
Bishop of Antioch, was not present and evidently did not want
to be. He was a close friend through a long correspondence
with Cyril, but he and Nestorius, who had come from Antioch
and had been educated there, were compatriots. John arrived
at the city a few days after the council began and settled his
personal quandary by setting up a rival council with his own
bishops. They issued a decree of deposition and of excommunication against Cyril and Memnon, the Bishop of Ephesus.
Another member of the hierarchy was also absent. Acacius,
Bishop of Beroea, was a man advanced in age but famous in
the East for his learning. He did not come at all and age was the
excuse. The correspondence with these two bishops is an important part of the letters. After the council was finally over, it
was Cyril's task to reconcile the bishops who had formed the
Conciliabulum with John and to restore peace in the churches
of the East. His joy in achieving this and in regaining his
friendship with John is seen in Letter 39.

(5) Certain of the letters are famed for their doctrinal content and accuracy. Letter 4, addressed to Nestorius, has been
called the dogmatic letter and was solemnly approved by the
Council of Ephesus as maintaining the teaching of Nicaea. The
Councils of Chalcedon in 451 and of Constantinople in 553 did
the same. Letter 17, sent to Nestorius by Cyril in the name of
the synod which he held at Alexandria in late 430, has twelve
anathemas at the end. It was added to the Acts of the Council
of Ephesus, although it was not formally approved by the
council. These three, namely Letters 4, 17, and 39 have been
called ecumenical.

(6) Almost the entire collection has to do with the Council of

Ephesus. There are no personal letters on everyday topics at all. Those which deal with the council fall into three groups. The first of these extends from Letter 1 to Letter 32, and is concerned with the beginning of the controversy and the results of it down to and including the council itself. The second group extends from Letter 33 to Letter 65, and is concerned with the question of John of Antioch and his bishops after the council, until peace was restored in the East. The third group extends from Letter 66 to Letter 74, and deals with the extension of the heresy; for, although some of the eastern bishops agreed to the deposition of Nestorius and the anathema against him, they began to maintain the ideas of Diodore of Tarsus and Theodore of Mopsuestia, the teachers of Nestorius.

(7) There are four administrative letters which Cyril wrote as Patriarch of Alexandria. These are 77, 78, 79, and 85. Two letters are prefaces to other works, namely 83 and 84. Letter 81 is against the teachings of Origen, and 82 is against the Messalians or Euchites. Two are out of place in regard to time, 75 and 76, which are to be dated at about 415. They deal with the restoration of the name of John Chrysostom to the diptychs. Two of the collection deal with the exegesis of passages in Sacred Scripture, 41, a long discussion of the word "scapegoat," and 80, an explanation of the punishment of Cain. This last one, however, is not Cyril's but a partial copy of Letter 260 of St. Basil.

(8) Certain letters are important for their doctrinal and theological content. These are 1, 4, 10, 11, 17, 39, 40, 44, 45, 46, 50 and 55. Some of these are unusually long, almost being small works in themselves, notably Letter 55.

(9) There is no single volume published which contains in one place the ancient texts of all of Cyril's letters as transmitted to us. The translation presented here is the first volume of such a work. (The Fathers of the Church will publish the remaining letters in the forthcoming Volume 77.) The largest collection is in Migne, 88 letters in Greek and Latin.[2] This is, for the most

---

2. J. P. Migne, ed., *S. P. N. Cyrilli Alexandriae Archiepiscopi Opera*, PG 76.385–390, 1065–1077; 77.9–390 (Paris, 1863, 1859).

part, a reprint of the Paris edition of 1638 by Joannes Aubert with added notes. One of these letters, 80, is not by Cyril, as stated above. Several are spurious. These are: 86 dealing with the date of Easter, 87 on the same topic and 88, a supposed letter from Hypatia to Cyril ending with an impossible statement that she wished to become a Nestorian Christian, although she was dead long before Nestorius was heretical.

(10) Information regarding the texts and whereabouts of Cyril's correspondence in Greek, Latin and other languages increased greatly with Geerard's publication in 1979 of the third volume of *Clavis Patrum Graecorum*. In this list of patristic writings Cyril's first letter is numbered as 5301 and the sequence continues to 5388. But in this translation these are numbered simply as Letters 1–88.[3] The notes for each letter contain the number assigned to it by Geerard for easy cross reference to the *Clavis Patrum Graecorum*. Geerard continued his numbering from 5389 to 5411 to include in his catalogue all the texts and fragments with their sources. In this translation Geerard 5389–5410 will be Letters 89–110. Geerard's number may be found in the notes for each letter. On Geerard 5411 see below, paragraph 21.

(11) Earlier in this century Schwartz published four letters previously unknown.[4] Lampe numbered these as Letters 89 to 92. Geerard changed the numbers which Lampe assigned.[5] Letters 89 and 90 were sent by Cyril to John of Antioch and from the contents in the sequence of time should come after Letter 39 not at the end of the collection. Likewise Letter 92 from Cyril to Acacius of Beroea, should come after Letter 32,

---

3. M. Geerard, ed., *Clavis Patrum Graecorum*, 4 vols. (Brepols-Turnhout, 1974–), 3(1979): 31–55. Geerard places Letters 6 and 7 under his entry 5306 and Letter 11(a) under his entry 5311. Consequently Letters 6 and 7, 8, 9, 10, 11, and 11(a) and the *CPG* number (less 5300) assigned to them by Geerard do not agree. Before Letters 6 and 7 and from Letter 12 onward, the *CPG* number (less 5300) and the number of the letter agree.

4. E. Schwartz, ed., *Acta Conciliorum Oecumenicorum* (Berlin and Leipzig, 1924–), 1.1.7 pp. 140–142, 152–153, 162–163.

5. G. W. H. Lampe, ed., *A Patristic Greek Lexicon* (Oxford, 1961), xxi. Geerard numbers Lampe's *ep.* 89 as 5392, *ep.* 90 as 5389, *ep.* 91 as 5390, and *ep.* 92 as 5393. See Geerard, *CPG*, 51–52.

and Letter 93 from Cyril to Maximian of Constantinople, should come after Letter 49.

(12) Schwartz also published the Greek text of Letter 32, which was previously known from the Latin version in Migne, and the Greek text of 33, also previously known from the Latin version in Migne, a fact not noted by Quasten.[6]

(13) Three letters, published by Schwartz, were inserted as appendices by the present translator. Appendix 1, from Pope Sixtus to Cyril, gave him instructions in handling the peace being arranged between the churches and approved Cyril's actions during the reign of Pope Celestine, whom Sixtus had recently succeeded. Chronologically this should come after Letter 32. Appendix 2, from John of Antioch to Cyril, should follow, just as Appendix 3, also from John of Antioch should come after Letter 35. These, although not written by Cyril, show how intensely the Pope was interested in religious affairs in the East and how much John of Antioch was trying to cooperate in the attainment of peace.

(14) The strangest document in the corpus of Cyril's correspondence is Letter 96, a *breve* or catalogue of treasures dispatched from Alexandria to Constantinople as bribes to influence the corrupt imperial court. It is so detailed that its genuine purport can scarcely be denied. Such actions, shocking as they are, seem to have become a custom in the reign of Theodosius II, who succeeded his father in 408 at the age of seven years and remained in power until 450. How this enormous number of gifts was brought to the capital is an unanswered question. The catalogue becomes more of a reality in the light of Appendix 4, a letter by Epiphanius, archdeacon and companion to Cyril and to Maximian, Bishop of Constantinople, which should be an introduction to Letter 96. The purpose of the bribes was to help in obtaining a decree of the emperor against Nestorius who had been condemned at the council.

(15) Appendix 5 is an alternate version of Letter 85, from

6. J. Quasten, *Patrology 3: The Golden Age of Patristic Literature from the Council of Nicaea to the Council of Chalcedon* (Utrecht-Antwerp, 1960; reprint Westminister, Md.: Christian Classics, 1983), 133.

Cyril to the bishops and synod at Carthage, dated before 428, in reply to a request for a copy of the decrees of the Council of Nicaea. Evidently the accurate records kept at Alexandria in Cyril's time were continuing the tradition which began with the founding of the city and its famous library.

(16) In 1933 C. Papadopoulos in his work on Cyril[7] gave a list of the letters classified according to date and time before or after an event, such as the Council of Ephesus. There are several corrections to be made. Letter 41 is not to Acacius of Melitene but to Acacius of Scythopolis. Letter 73 is not to Rabbula of Edessa but from him to Cyril, and Cyril's canonical letter is not 46 but 78, just as it was composed not before 446 but before 444, the year of Cyril's death. Papadopoulos only dealt with the letters composed by Cyril. Others were omitted. It would indeed be tempting to take all the letters in the correspondence, either by or to Cyril, and arrange them in chronological order disregarding all previous systems of numbering. Papadopoulos did this with the ones written by Cyril, but to do it to all letters and fragments would only confuse the scholar. Consequently, for those who would wish to read in chronological order, the following is offered based on the work of Papadopoulos.

DATES OF LETTERS

Before 428.
Letters 75, 76, and 85.

Between the years 428 to 431.
Letters 1, 110, 100, 2 to 19, 106 to 109, and 84.

During the Council of Ephesus, 431.
Letters 20 to 24, 95, and 25 to 30 inclusive.

After the Council from Alexandria.
94, Appendix 4, 96, 31 and 32.

---

7. C. Papadopoulos, *Ho Hagios Kurillos Alexandreias* (Alexandria, 1933), 454.

During negotiations with the eastern bishops.
Letters 92, Appendix 1 and 2, 33, 34, 35,
Appendix 3, 36, 39, 89 and 90.

After the reconciliation, 433 to 435.
Letters 37, 38, 40 to 49, 93, 50 to 54,
56, 57, 58, 102, 103, 104, 105.

During discussion about Theodore of Mopsuestia.
Letters 55, and 59 to 74.

At an uncertain date on different subjects.
Letters 56, 77, 78, 79, 81, 82 and 83.

Fragments, after 428.
97 to 99.

Spurious.
Letters 86, 87, 88, and perhaps 91 and 101.

Incorrectly included in Cyril's corpus.
Letter 80 by Basil the Great.

(17) To aid the reader it seemed best to place the identification of the principal persons named in the correspondence in one place. For many of the minor characters mention in the letters is the only item of identification known about them. Hence it did not appear suitable to include them.

NAME	EPISCOPAL SEE	DATES
Acacius	Beroea	c. 322 to c. 433
Acacius	Melitene	? to c. 438
Acacius	Scythopolis	
Alexander	Alexandria	? to 328
Amphilochius	Iconium	c. 340–345 to 395
Apollinaris	Laodicea	c. 310 to c. 390
Athanasius	Alexandria	295 to 373
Atticus	Constantinople	? to 425
Aurelius	Carthage	? to c. 430

Basil	Caesarea in Cappadocia	c. 330 to 379
Beronicianus	Tyre	
Calosyrius	Arsinoë	
Celestine I	Rome, Pope 422–432	? to 432
Cyril	Alexandria	? to 444
Diodore	Tarsus	? to c. 392
Domnus	Antioch	
Dorotheus	Marcianopolis (titular)	
Dynatos	Nikopolis in Epiros	
Epictetus	Corinth	
Eunomius	Cyzicus	? to after 394
Eutherius	Tyana in Cappadocia	
Firmus	Caesarea in Cappadocia	? to 439
Flavian	Antioch	381 to 404
Flavian	Philippi	
Gregory	Nazianzus	c. 330 to c. 389
Gregory	Nyssa	c. 335 to 394
Helladius	Tarsus	
John	Antioch	? to 441
John Chrysostom	Constantinople	344–354 to 405
Juvenal	Jerusalem	? to 458
Maximian	Constantinople	
Memnon	Ephesus	
Mosaeus	Antaradus in Syria	
Nectarius	Constantinople	? to 397
Nestorius	Constantinople	c. 381 to 450
Paul	Emesa	
Proclus	Constantinople	? to 446
Rabbula	Edessa	? to 435
Rufus	Thessalonica	

Sixtus III	Rome, Pope	
	432–440	? to 440
Succensus	Diocaesarea in	
	Isauria	
Theodore	Mopsuestia	c. 350 to 428
Theodoret	Cyrus	c. 393 to c. 466
Theodotus	Ancyra	? to 445
Theophilus	Alexandria	? to 412
Valerian	Iconium	

(18) The Roman emperor was Theodosius II whose reign extended from 408 to 450. He was born in 401 and died in 450. Aristolaus was a tribune and secretary at court. Candidianus is mentioned in Letter 23 as a count of the court. The same name is given to a deacon in Letter 29. Another count named John is mentioned in Letter 28.

(19) The style of the letters in keeping with the content is serious. In them we are introduced to the superlatives of proper address among prelates of that time. They may seem extreme to us, but it is to be noted that they are used about Nestorius until he was condemned and deposed. Then they cease. The sense of dignity which they show indicates the serious regard implicit in them and the gravity of the communication.

(20) Cyril's famous formula, which was misunderstood and employed by the Monophysites after his death, appears in Letter 45. A statement close to it appears in Letter 40. He can only be clearly understood, however, by a careful reading of the context in which the expression is found. Cyril at all times strongly maintained the traditional doctrine of the Council of Nicaea as is seen by perusing the doctrinal letters. The height to which he goes in thought and expression presents challenging reading for the student of theology.

(21) Geerard listed as 5411 a letter to a bishop who asked for commentaries on Paul's letters. It evidently is preserved in a manuscript at Mount Athos, but has been omitted here, since it has not yet been published.

LETTERS

1–50

LETTER 1

Cyril, to the priests and deacons, fathers of monks and to those practicing the solitary life with you who are firm in faith in God, beloved and most dear; greetings in the Lord.[1]

OME OF YOUR brethren, as it is the custom, arrived in Alexandria. I asked and very eagerly inquired whether you yourselves are striving to excel in true and blameless faith, walking in the footsteps of your fathers' gentleness, and are distinguishing yourselves in that excellent way of life, and whether you yourselves highly esteem the toils of your religious training by considering it truly a joy to choose suffering nobly for the sake of the good.

(2) They reported that you are so disposed, and added that you are competing rather zealously with the manly deeds of your predecessors. Therefore, I rejoiced of necessity and my spirit was diffused with contentment, claiming as my own the good repute of my children, and very appropriately. And it is not unheard of that gymnastic trainers exult in the strength of the young and, if they achieve anything which redounds to the praise of their training, they ascribe this to themselves as a crown on their brows, and appropriate the glories of their pupils' manliness. It would, indeed, be strange for me, your spiritual father, not to be filled with divine gladness of heart, no less than they, spurring you on with words to your noble endeavor so that you might carry off the prize after you have overcome the movements of the flesh, and by prayer have

1. For the critical text of this letter see Schwartz, *ACO* 1.1.1 pp. 10–23. Geerard numbers this letter 5301 in *CPG*. See also A. J. Festugière, *Éphèse et Chalcédoine Actes des Conciles* (Paris, 1982), 27–44.

avoided falling into sin and being defeated by satan's temptations.

(3) Surely, then, just as the disciple of the Savior says, "Do you on your part strive diligently to supply your faith with virtue, your virtue with knowledge, your knowledge with self-control, your self-control with patience, your patience with piety, your piety with fraternal love, your fraternal love with charity. For if these virtues are present in you and abound in you, they render you neither inactive nor unfruitful in the knowledge of our Lord Jesus Christ."[2] For I say that those who have chosen to live the glorious and beloved way of life devised by Christ must first be adorned with simple and unblemished faith, and so then add virtue to their faith. When this has been done, they must strive to enrich their knowledge of the mystery of Christ and ascend to the most complete understanding of him. For this, I think is "to attain unto a perfect man" and to come "unto the measure of the age of his fullness."[3] With the sobriety, therefore, proper to monks, fight manfully against spiritual and, at the same time, physical disturbances, with loins well girt.[4] In this way, you shall be radiant and glorious even with the beauty of the hope prepared for the saints. Above all, let your faith be true and sincere and completely without reproach. For, in this way, you yourselves also, by following the pious example of your holy fathers, shall take up your abode in the mansions above and shall live in the heavenly dwellings. Of these also the prophet Isaiah makes mention saying, "Your eyes shall see Jerusalem; it is a wealthy city, and may its tents not be shaken."[5]

(4) Therefore, how would it be that I do not know that your way of life is illustrious and admirable and that your true and sincere faith rests on a secure foundation? But I am disturbed beyond measure because I have heard that certain troublesome rumors have reached you, and that certain men go about destroying your simple faith, spewing out a multitude of useless pet phrases, making close inquiries, and saying that it is

---

2. Cf. 2 Pt 1.5–8.
3. Eph 4.13.

4. Cf. Ex 12.11; Lk 12.35.
5. Cf. Is 33.20.

necessary to specify clearly whether or not the Holy Virgin Mary is to be called the Mother of God.[6] It would be better for you to pay no attention at all to such inquiries and not at all to dig up difficult questions which are seen, as it were, in a mirror and are a puzzle for keen minds and trained intellects. For the finer distinctions of speculations transcend the comprehension of the less instructed. However, you have not remained completely ignorant of such discussions and it is likely that some choose to be fond of disputing and of fixing this mischief like a stake into those whose minds are not firmly made up. Hence, I thought it necessary to say some few words to you concerning these matters. I do not do this that you may have a greater battle of words; rather, I intend that you may escape the danger of going astray if anyone should spring up with an attack on the truth with random words. I write that you may assist others as brothers, besides, by the proper reasonings, persuading them to maintain as a precious pearl in their own souls the divine faith handed down from above by the apostles to the churches.

(5) Therefore, I am amazed if some should question at all whether the Holy Virgin should be called the Mother of God. For if our Lord Jesus Christ is God, how is the Holy Virgin who bore him not the Mother of God? The inspired disciples transmitted this faith to us, even if they have not made mention of the term. So we have been taught to think by the holy Fathers.

(6) And, in any event, our father Athanasius, of hallowed memory, adorned the throne of the Church of Alexandria for the whole of forty-six years and arrayed an unconquerable and apostolic knowledge in battle against the sophistries of the unholy heretics and greatly gladdened the world by his writings as by a most fragrant perfume and all bear witness to the accuracy and piety of his teachings.

---

6. Θεοτόκος in Greek, "God-bearing." The meaning of this title was an important part of the controversy. See P. Imhof and B. Lorenz, *Maria Theotokos bei Cyrill von Alexandrien: zur Theotokos-Tradition und ihrer Relevanz; eine dogmengeschichtliche Untersuchung zur Verwendung des Wortes Theotokos bei Cyrill von Alexandrien vor dem Konzil von Ephesus unter Berücksichtigung von Handschriften der direkten Überlieferung* (Munich, 1981).

(7) When he composed for us his work concerning the holy and consubstantial Trinity, in the third book from the beginning to the end, he called the Holy Virgin the Mother of God. I shall, of necessity, use his own very words which are as follows: "Therefore the mark and characteristic of Holy Scripture, as we have often said, is this that it contains a twofold declaration concerning the Savior, that he both always was God and that he is the Son, being the Word and brightness and wisdom[7] of the Father, and that afterwards, for our sake, by taking flesh from the Virgin Mary, the Mother of God, he became man."[8]

(8) And after other matters he says again, "In truth there have been many saints and men cleansed of all sin. For both Jeremiah was sanctified from the womb,[9] and John, as yet unborn, leaped for joy at the voice of Mary, the Mother of God."[10]

(9) Athanasius, therefore, is a man worthy of trust and deserving of confidence, since he did not say anything which is not in agreement with Holy Scripture. For how would so brilliant and celebrated a man stray from the truth, one who was so admired by all even in that holy and great council, I mean the one at Nicaea, which was assembled in critical times. He did not yet hold the office of bishop, but rather belonged to the class of clerics and yet, because of his sagacity and gentleness besides, and because of his exceedingly subtle and incomparable mind, he was, at that time, taken as his companion by Alexander, the bishop of happy memory. He was as close to the old man as a son is to his father, leader in everything helpful, and the one who showed the way right well in all things which were to be done.

(10) Since it is likely that some think it necessary for us to confirm our statement concerning this matter from the holy and divinely inspired Scripture itself, and assert besides that the holy and great council mentioned above neither said that

7. Cf. Heb 1.3 and 1 Cor. 1.31.
8. A quotation from Athanasius, *Contra Arianos* 3.29. (PG 26.385–388).
9. Cf. Jer 1.5.
10. Cf. Lk 1.44, 45. The quotation is from *Contra Arianos* 3.33. (PG 26.393–396).

the Mother of the Lord is the Mother of God, nor in truth
defined any such thing, come now, let us show as far as possible
in what way the mystery of the economy of salvation devised by
Christ has been announced to us by Holy Scripture. Then,
also, what the Fathers themselves have spoken who set forth
the standard of blameless faith, since the Holy Spirit taught
them the truth; for, according to our Savior's words, it was not
they themselves who spoke but "the Spirit of God and Father
who speaks through them."[11] For when it has been shown thus
that the one born of the Holy Virgin is God according to
nature, I think that, necessarily, no one at all will shrink from
thinking, and also saying, that she should be called the Mother
of God and very rightly.

(11) Thus runs the Creed of our faith. "We believe in one
God, the Father almighty, creator of all things visible and
invisible, and in one Lord, Jesus Christ, the Son of God, the
only begotten of the Father, that is from his substance, God of
God, light of light, true God of true God, begotten not made,
consubstantial with the Father, through whom all things were
made both in heaven and on earth, who for us men and for our
salvation descended, became incarnate, was made man, suffered, and rose again on the third day, ascended into heaven
and is coming to judge the living and the dead; and in the Holy
Spirit."[12]

(12) Now the inventors of heresies, digging pits of perdition
for themselves and of ruin for others, have slipped to the point
of thinking and saying that the Son is recent, and was produced by God the Father just like creatures. The wretches do
not blush to circumscribe with a beginning in time him who is
before every age and time, rather who is the maker of the ages.
In their teaching they draw the Son down from the equality
and glory with God the Father. They barely concede to him
preexistence before others, and say that he has an intermedi-
ate position between God and man, neither sharing the infinite
glory nor being hemmed in by the limitations of creation.

11. Mt. 10.20.
12. This is the Nicene Creed.

(13) Who, then, is this one cast down from his divine preeminence and removed from the limitations of creation? The matter is completely inconceivable and there is no discernible place or manner of speaking of someone in between creator and creation. Although they dislodged him from the throne of divinity, they have arrived at a point in their teaching that they call him the Son and God, and think that he is to be adored although the law openly proclaims, "The Lord your God shall you worship and him only shall you serve,"[13] and although God said to the Israelites through the voice of David, "There shall be no new god among you, nor shall you adore a foreign god."[14]

(14) But like those that left the well-trodden highway of the truth, they hasten into holes and rocks and, as Solomon says, "They have diverted their paths to wander from their own vineyard and bring fruitlessness to their hands."[15] But we into whose minds the light of God has shone, having chosen to think what is incomparably better than their nonsense, and following the faith of the holy Fathers, say that the Son, in a divine and ineffable manner, was truly begotten of the substance of God the Father, and that he is known in his own person, that he is one with him who has begotten him in identity of substance,[16] and that he is in him, and, in turn, has the Father in him.[17] We confess that the Son is light from light, God from God according to nature, equal in glory and equal in operation, the image and brightness,[18] being equal in every respect whatsoever, and inferior in no manner. For thus, with the addition of the Holy Spirit, the holy and consubstantial Trinity is united in one divine nature.

(15) Now, the inspired Scripture says that the Word of God was made flesh,[19] that is, that he was united to flesh which had a

---

13. Mt 4.10; Dt 6.13.
14. Cf. Ps 80(81).10. Cyril quotes the Septuagint text, as frequently hereafter.
15. Cf. Prv 9.12b, c (LXX).
16. Cf. Jn 10.30.   18. Cf. Heb 1.3.
17. Cf. Jn 14.10.   19. Cf. Jn 1.14.

rational soul.[20] Following the teachings of the Gospels, the holy and great council said that he is begotten of the substance of God and Father as the only begotten, "through whom and in whom all things are,"[21] for us men and for our salvation he descended from heaven, was made flesh and became man, suffered and rose, and that in due time he shall come as judge, and it named the Word of God one Lord Jesus Christ. Note well, then, how when saying that the Son was one and naming him the Lord Jesus Christ, they say that he was begotten of God the Father, that he is the only begotten, and God from God, light from light, begotten not made, and consubstantial with the Father.

(16) And yet, someone may say, we shall find the name Christ[22] applied not to Emmanuel alone, but also applied to others. For God said somewhere[23] about those chosen and sanctified by the Spirit, "Touch not my anointed ones, and to my prophets do no harm."[24] Nay more, the divinely inspired David calls Saul who had been anointed as king by God through the hand of Samuel,[25] the "Lord's anointed."[26] And why do I mention this when it is possible for those who desire to look at the matter calmly to see that those who have been justified by faith in Christ and have been sanctified in the Spirit are honored by such a name? And therefore, the prophet Habacuc has foretold the mystery of Christ and salvation through him saying, "You went forth for the salvation of your people, for the salvation of your anointed ones."[27]

(17) Consequently, the name Christ would not be applicable exclusively and properly to Emmanuel, as I said, but also to all the rest who may have been anointed with the grace of the

---

20. This stipulation is against the heresy of Apollinaris who denied that Christ had a rational soul.

21. Cf. Col 1.16, 17.

22. It is important for this passage to remember that the word "Christ" means "the Anointed One."

23. This sign of vagueness in quoting a text is not unusual for ancient writers, both pagan and Christian, who often quoted from memory.

24. Ps 104(105).15.   26. 1 Sm (1 Kgs) 24.7.

25. Cf. 1 Sm (1 Kgs) 16.13.   27. Cf. Hb 3.13.

Holy Spirit. For the word is derived from the action, and the name anointed from the fact of having been anointed. That we ourselves, too, are very rich in a grace so illustrious and truly precious the learned John confirms saying, "And you have an anointing from the Holy One";[28] and again, "You have no need that anyone teach you, but his anointing teaches you."[29] Concerning Emmanuel Scripture records, "how God anointed Jesus of Nazareth with the Holy Spirit and with power."[30] The inspired David says to him, "You have loved justice and hated iniquity, therefore God, your God, has anointed you with the oil of gladness above your companions."[31] What, therefore, would anyone see extraordinary in the Holy Virgin compared with other women, even if it were said that she bore the Emmanuel? For it would not be paradoxical even if one chose to call the mother of each of the anointed christ-bearer.

(18) But there is a great gap separating our condition even by immeasurable differences from the glory and preeminence of our Savior. For we are servants, but he, by nature, is Lord and God, even if he was among us and in our nature according to the dispensation of the Incarnation. For this reason, the blessed Paul called him Christ and God, speaking as follows, "For know this and understand that no fornicator, or unclean person, or coveteous one who is an idolater, has any inheritance in the kingdom of Christ and God."[32] Consequently, all the others, as I said, may be anointed ones, and very reasonably, because of having been anointed, but Christ alone is true God, the Emmanuel. And in reality, one would not err if he chose to say that the mothers of the others were christ-bearers, but in no way god-bearers also. The Holy Virgin alone in contrast with them is considered and called both Mother of Christ and Mother of God. For she has borne, not a mere man as we are, but rather the Word of God the Father made flesh, and become man. For we, too, were called gods[33] according to grace, but the Son of God is not God in this way, rather he is

---

28. 1 Jn 2.20.
29. 1 Jn 2.27.
30. Acts 10.38.

31. Cf. Ps 44(45).8.
32. Cf. Eph 5.5.
33. Cf. Ps 81(82).6; Jn 10.34.

God according to nature and in truth, even though he was made flesh.

(19) But perhaps you will say this, "Tell me, then, is the Virgin the Mother of his divinity?" And in reply to this we say that his living and subsistent Word was begotten admittedly from the very substance of God and from the Father, and that what was without beginning had a beginning in time, always having existed with his begetter, in him and with him coexisting and coplanning, and that upon the completion of the appointed time when he became flesh, that is, when he was united to flesh having a rational soul,[34] that Scripture states he was born of a woman according to the flesh also.

(20) The mystery of his Incarnation in a way is like to our being born. For the mothers of those on earth, subject to nature's laws regarding birth, have flesh implanted in their wombs which little by little grows according to certain unseen operations of God, coming to maturity in human form. God sends the spirit for a living being in a manner known to him. This is according to the saying of the prophet, "for he forms the spirit of man in him."[35] The logos of the body is one and, likewise, that of the soul is another. Yet even if these women are only the mothers of the bodies of those upon earth, nevertheless they bear a whole living being, one, I mean, consisting of body and soul. They are not said to bear only a part of it. No one would say that Elizabeth,[36] for example, was the mother of only a body and not the one who brought a soul into the world besides. For she bore the Baptist,[37] a man endowed with a soul and as one living being consisting of both, I mean a man having both a soul and a body.

(21) We will accept that something such as this was effected at the birth of the Emmanuel, too. For his only begotten Word, as I said, was begotten from the substance of God the Father.

34. Cf. n. 20.
35. Cf. Zec 12.1.
36. Nestorius also used Elizabeth and her son in argument as an example. See F. Loofs, *Nestoriana: Die Fragmente des Nestorius gesammelt, untersucht und herausgegeben* (Halle, 1905), 352.
37. Cf. Lk 1.57.

But after the Word assumed flesh and made it his own, he also bears the name Son of man and became like us. It is in no way absurd to say, I think, but rather necessary to confess also that he was born according to the flesh from a woman, just as, of course, the soul of a man is generated together with its own body and is considered as one with it, even though in nature it is known in comparison with the body to be different and existing by itself according to its own logos. And if someone wished to say that the mother of someone is the mother of a body but not the one who brought a soul into the world, he is thinking extremely foolishly. For a living being is born, as I said, skillfully composed of unlike principles, from two, indeed, but one man results, each principle remaining that which it is, both brought together as if into one natural unity and so joined with each other that each communicates to the other what is proper to itself.

(22) That the unity in Christ is very, very necessary is entirely without difficulty and easy to perceive through many other arguments. For come, if you please, let us inquire closely into the words of blessed Paul, paying attention as meticulously as possible. Now he said about the only begotten, "Who being in the form of God, did not consider equality with God to be robbery, but emptied himself, taking the form of a servant, and being made like unto men; and appearing in the form of man, he humbled himself."[38] Now who is this one "being in the form of God and not having considered equality with God to be robbery"? Or how has he emptied himself? How did he descend to humiliation and in the form of a servant? Now there are some who cut the one Lord Jesus Christ in two, that is, into man and into the Word of God the Father. They say that the one born of the Holy Virgin submitted to the emptying. They differentiate the Word of God the Father from him. Let them prove that in form and in equality he[39] is considered and, in fact, is from the Father, in order that he might submit to the manner of emptying himself, to which

38. Phil 2.6–8.
39. i.e., Mary's Son as separate from the Word.

very position he had not attained. But there is no creature, if considered according to its own nature, which is equal to the Father. How, then, is he said to have emptied himself, if, being man by nature, he has been born like us from a woman? And tell me the nature of the higher eminence greater than that of human from which he descended to be man? Or how might he be considered to have taken the form of a servant, which he did not have to start with, who by nature belonged to the class of servants and lay under the yokes of servitude?

(23) But they say that he who is by nature and truly the free Son, the Word of God the Father, God in the form of his begetter and equal to him, dwelt in a man born of a woman, and this is the emptying, and the issue of the humiliation and the humbling of himself in the form of a servant.[40] Moreover, my dear friends, would indwelling alone in a man on the part of the Word of God suffice for the emptying of himself?

(24) And is it safe to say that thus he put on the form of a servant and that this would be the manner of his humiliation, even though He says to the holy apostles, as I hear, "If anyone loves me, he will keep my word, and my Father will love him, and we will come to him and make our abode with him"?[41] Do you hear how he said that he and God the Father will make their abode in those who love him? Therefore, shall we concede that God the Father also emptied himself, and that he endured an emptying of himself similar to the Son's, and that he assumed the form of a servant because he makes the holy souls of those who love him his own abode?

(25) What of the Holy Spirit indwelling in us? Does he fulfill the plan of the Incarnation which we say was carried out by the Son alone for the sake of the salvation and life of all men? Away with such extravagant and entirely senseless rashness!

(26) Therefore, the Word, though being in the form and equality of God the Father, humbled himself when, being made flesh as John says,[42] he was born of a woman, and having a begetting from God the Father, he also endured to experi-

40. Cf. Phil 2.5–7.
41. Jn 14.23.
42. Cf. Jn 1.14.

ence a birth like ours for our sake. Otherwise, let them explain
how the Word of God the Father would be known and called
Christ by us. If he bears the name Christ from the anointing,
then whom has the Father anointed with the oil of gladness,[43]
that is, with the Holy Spirit? If, therefore, they say it is true that
the one anointed is the Word who is God, and properly, his
only begotten Son, they do not see how they do violence to the
nature of the only begotten and misinterpret the mystery of
the Incarnation.

(27) For if the Word, being God, has been anointed with the
Holy Spirit, they will also admit, not willingly of course, that he
was by all means in need of sanctification in the ages in which
he existed previously, during which he had not yet been
anointed, for he did not yet have a share in the gift given to him
later. But that which is bereft of sanctification is changeable by
nature and would not be thought of as entirely free from sin or
the power to err. Therefore, the Word has taken a turn for the
better, perhaps. How, then, is he the same and not changed?
And if the Word, though being God both by form and by
equality to the Father, was anointed and sanctified, someone
might say, perhaps, like a person carried off course from this
matter to foolish ideas, that perhaps somehow the Father
himself needed sanctification also, for the Son now appears
much greater than the Father, if the Son himself has been
sanctified, for the Son was equal to the Father in form before
the Son's sanctification. But the Father has remained as he
always was, and is, and shall be, having received no additional
endowment for betterment through sanctification in the same
way as the Son. And the Spirit, the one sanctifying them, is seen
to be better than both, if, as is the fact, "Beyond all contradic-
tion, that which is less is blessed by the superior."[44] But this is
nonsense and claptrap and the charges of madness. For the
consubstantial Trinity is holy by nature. The Father is holy,
and the Son is substantially and equally holy, and the Spirit in
the same way. Surely, then, insofar as his own nature is con-

43. Cf. Ps 44(45).8.
44. Heb 7.7.

cerned, the Word of God the Father has not been sanctified separately.

(28) But if anyone should think that the one born of the Holy Virgin was anointed and sanctified alone[45] and, for this reason, is called Christ, let him come forward and say whether the anointing is enough to prove that the one anointed is equal in glory and shares the throne with God who is over all. And if the anointing is sufficient, and they shall say that this is true, we also have been anointed. And the inspired John will bear witness saying, "But you have an anointing from the Holy One."[46] Therefore, perhaps somehow, even we ourselves will be equal to God, and nothing at all, I think, prevents us from also sitting beside him, in the same way doubtless as the Emmanuel himself. For these words were addressed to him, "Sit at my right hand, until I make your enemies your footstool."[47] Let the holy throng of spirits above worship us also. For Scripture says, "When he brings the firstborn into the world, he says, 'And let all the angels of God adore him.'"[48] But we, even though we have been anointed with the Holy Spirit and are very rich because of the grace of adoption as sons and are even called gods,[49] will not be ignorant of the due limits of our nature. For we are from the earth and belong among the servants. But he is not in the condition in which we are, but by nature is truly the Son and Lord of all and from heaven.

(29) And, surely, we who have chosen to think aright do not say that God became the Father of flesh; nor, again, that the nature of the divinity was born of a woman with the humanity not yet assumed. But rather, bringing together into unity the Word begotten of God and the man perfectly born of the Holy Virgin, we will adore one Christ and Lord, Jesus, neither placing him outside the bounds of divinity because of his flesh, nor bringing him down into mere humanity because of his likeness to us. In this way, you will understand that the Word begotten of God endured a voluntary emptying; in this way, he

45. Cf. n. 39.
46. 1 Jn 2.20.
47. Ps 109(110).1.

48. Heb 1.6.
49. Cf. n. 33.

humbled himself by taking the form of a servant,[50] he who, according to his own nature, was free; in this way he, "assumed descent from Abraham,"[51] and the Word of God has partaken of blood and flesh.[52] For if he is considered mere man as we are, how did he assume descent from Abraham as something by nature different from himself? How is he said to have partaken of their flesh in order that "he should in all things be made like unto his brethren"?[53] For what is said to be made like to something moves from dissimilarity to what it must resemble.

(30) Accordingly, the Word of God assumed descent from Abraham and "has blood and flesh in common"[54] by having made his own the body born from a woman, in order that, being not only God but having become man as well, he might be known among us by this union. Accordingly, the Emmanuel is admittedly of two entities, of divinity and humanity. There is, however, one Lord Jesus Christ and one Son truly, God and man at the same time; not a man made divine who is equal to those who are made divine according to grace, but rather true God who has appeared in human form for our sake. The inspired Paul will confirm this for us when he says, "But when the fullness of time came, God sent his Son, born of a woman, born under the law, that he might redeem those who were under the law, that we might receive the adoption of sons."[55] Who is the one, then, sent under the law, born of a woman, as he said, except him who is beyond laws as God, but, since he was called man after his birth, was also under the law, in order that "he should in all things be made like unto his brethren."[56] And, therefore, he paid the didrachma along with Peter according to the law of Moses.[57] But because as the Son he is free and as God superior to the law, even if as man he was born under the law, he instructed him saying, "From whom do the kings of the earth receive tribute or customs; from their own sons, or from others?" But when Peter said, "From others," he

50. Cf. Phil 2.6–8.
51. Cf. Heb 2.16.
52. Cf. Heb 2.14.
53. Cf. Heb 2.17.

54. Heb 2.14.
55. Cf. Gal 4.4, 5.
56. Heb 2.17.
57. Cf. Mt 17.26.

concluded, "The sons then are exempt."[58] Consequently it is clear that the Word begotten of God, existing outside the flesh and separately, so to speak, would not be called the Christ. That such a name was appropriate for him when he became man, by taking the proofs out of Holy Scripture itself, let us show that he is God according to nature even though his divinity has been brought into union, I say, with flesh of his own. Once this truth has been made clear, the Holy Virgin may be called the Mother of God by us, and very rightly.

(31) Accordingly, the prophet Isaiah points out beforehand the Son well-nigh incarnate and soon to come, in the words, "You feeble hands and weak knees, be strong; you faint-hearted in purpose, urge yourselves on; be strong, and fear not; behold, our God is rendering judgment, and will render it; God himself will come and save us. Then shall the eyes of the blind be opened, and the ears of the deaf shall hear; then shall the lame man leap like a stag, and the stammering tongue shall be clear."[59] Observe how he names him Lord[60] and calls him God, seeing that he speaks in the Spirit; note that he knew the Emmanuel would not be simply a man bearing God nor, of a truth, as one assumed as an agent, but knew that he was truly God and incarnate. For then, then the eyes of the blind were opened, and the ears of the deaf heard, and the lame man leaped as a hart, and the tongue of the dumb became free. Thus, the Holy Spirit bade the holy evangelists to proclaim him saying, "Go up onto a high mountain, you that bring good tidings to Sion; lift up your voice with strength, you that bring good tidings to Jerusalem; lift it up, fear not. To the cities of Juda say: behold your God; behold, the Lord comes with strength, and his arm with authority; behold, his reward is with him and his work is before him. He shall feed his flock like a shepherd, he shall gather together the lambs in his arm."[61] For our Lord Jesus Christ showed himself to us having divine strength, and his arm with authority, that is, with power and dominion. For that very reason, He said to the leper, "I will; be

---

58. Cf. Mt 17.25, 26.
59. Cf. Is 35.3–6.

60. Cf. Is 35.2.
61. Cf. Is 40.9–11.

made clean."[62] For that reason, he touched the bier and raised up the dead son of the widow.[63]

(32) And he gathered together the lambs for he is the good shepherd who laid down his life for his sheep. For this reason, he said, "Even as the Father knows me and I know the Father; and I lay down my life for my sheep. And other sheep I have that are not of this fold. Them also I must bring, and they shall hear my voice, and there shall be one fold and one shepherd."[64] At the beginning of his preaching about him, the inspired John the Baptist proclaimed him to the people throughout all Judaea, neither as an agent of divinity nor even simply as a man bearing God, as some say, but rather God in union with flesh, that is, made man, saying, "Make ready the way of the Lord, make straight the paths of our God."[65] Whose ways did he command to be made ready, except those of Christ, that is, of the Word made manifest in the form of man? And the inspired Paul too, in my opinion, gives sufficient evidence for [our] faith when he bears witness in these words, "What then shall we say? If God is for us, who is against us? He who has not spared even his own Son, but has delivered him for us all, how can he fail to grant us also all things with him?"[66] Then, tell me, how may the one born of the Holy Virgin be considered God's own Son? Because just as that which has been born of man according to nature is a man's own child, indeed, this is true of all other living beings, so he, too, is considered to be and is called God's own Son begotten of his substance. How, therefore, is Christ, who was delivered up by God the Father for the salvation and life of all, called God's own Son? For "he was delivered up for our sins,"[67] and "he himself bore the sins of many in his body upon the tree,"[68] according to the words of the prophet. Now this is already evident, since the fact of the union, necessarily admitted, proves that the very Son of God is Emmanuel who was born of the Holy Virgin. For his body was not that of someone else like us, but rather the body born from

62. Mt 8.3.
63. Cf. Lk 7.12–15.
64. Jn 10.15, 16.
65. Cf. Mt 3.3.

66. Cf. Rom 8.31, 32.
67. Cf. Rom 4.25.
68. Cf. 1 Pt 2.24; Is 53.12.

her is the very body of the Word himself who is from the Father.

(33) But if anyone assigns to him only the mere rendering of service as an instrument, even though unwillingly, he will also deprive him of being truly the Son. Come now, for the sake of argument, let it be assumed that there is a man, who has a son skilled with the lyre and trained to play the best composi- tions. Will such a man classify the lyre, which is the instrument of song, in the category of a son and identical with his son? How is this anything but the height of folly? For the lyre was used as an indication of his skill, but he is the son of his father even though separated from his instrument. But if they should then say that he who was born of a woman was used as an instrument that wonders might be performed through him, and to add luster to the message of the inspired evangelists, let each of the holy prophets also be called an instrument of divinity, and Moses, the teacher of sacred truths above all others. He lifted up his rod and turned rivers into blood.[69] He separated the sea itself and bade the people of Israel to pass through the midst of it.[70] He struck his rod against rocks and made them the sources of water and showed that the flint was a spring.[71] He was both mediator between God and men[72] and servant of the law and led the people. Therefore, there was nothing extraordinary in Christ, and in no way did he surpass those born before him, if he himself is used in the capacity and function of an instrument in the same way as Moses. And the inspired David has prated utter nonsense in all likelihood, when he states that he had such advantages, saying "Who among the clouds will be compared to the Lord; or who will be like unto the Lord among the sons of God?"[73]

(34) But the very wise Paul proves Moses functioning among the servants, but calls Christ God and Lord, who was born of a woman according to the divine plan, that is, Christ. For he has written as follows, "Therefore, holy brethren, par-

69. Cf. Ex 7.19, 20.
70. Cf. Ex 14.21, 22.
71. Cf. Ex 17.6.

72. Cf. 1 Tm 2.5; Gal 3.19.
73. Cf. Ps 88(89).7.

takers of a heavenly calling, consider the apostle and high priest of our confession, Jesus, who is faithful to him who made him, as was Moses also in all his house.[74] For he was deemed worthy of greater glory than Moses, just as the builder of a house has greater glory than the house that he built. For every house is built by someone; but he who created all things is God. And Moses indeed was faithful in all his house as a servant, to testify concerning those things that were to be spoken; but Christ is faithful as the Son over his own house, of whose house we are."[75] Note well, therefore, how Paul has preserved both the measure of Christ's humanity and assigns to him the preeminence of the highest glory and of divine dignity. In calling him high priest and apostle, and affirming, moreover, that he is faithful to him who made him, he says that he surpasses Moses in honor as much as a builder surpasses the fame of his building. Then, he continues, "For every house is built by someone; but he who created all things is God." Accordingly, the inspired Moses is placed among created beings and structures, but Christ has been shown as creator of all things even though God is said to have created everything.[76] Therefore, he is indubitably also true God. "And Moses, indeed, was faithful in all his house as a servant, but Christ is faithful as the Son over his own house, of whose house we are." And moreover, as God says through the voice of the prophets, "I will dwell and move among them, and I will be their God and they shall be my people."[77]

(35) Someone, perhaps, may say, "But who would know the difference between Christ and Moses, if both were born through a woman? How is the one a servant and faithful in the house, but the other, as the Son, is Lord by nature over his house, which we are?" But I think that this matter is manifest to everyone who is good in heart and has the mind of Christ, as blessed Paul says.[78] For the one was man and under the yoke of

74. Cf. Nm 12.8.
75. Cf. Heb 3.1–6.
76. Cf. Jn 1.3.
77. 2 Cor 6.16; cf. Lv 26.11, 12; also Ez 37.26, 27.
78. Cf. 1 Cor 7.40.

servitude, but the other was free by nature as God and creator of all, and endured a willing emptying for us.[79] But this will not banish him from his divine glory, nor keep him from his most excellent preeminence over all; how can it be! We have been enriched with his Spirit, for his Spirit has come to dwell in our hearts,[80] and have taken our place among the children of God, and yet have not lost being what we are. For we are men according to nature even though we say to God, "Abba! Father!"[81] Similarly he, God the Word, ineffably begotten of the substance of God and the Father, in assuming his humanity, has honored that nature, but has not departed from his preeminence, but has remained God in his humanity. Therefore, we do not say that the temple born of the Virgin was used as an instrument. Rather, following the faith of the Holy Scripture and the words of the saints, we shall be assured that the Word was made flesh in the ways very often previously explained by us. He also laid down his life for us. For since his death was the salvation of the world, he endured the cross, despising shame,[82] even though he was life according to nature, as God. How, then, is life said to die? By life suffering death in his own flesh, in order that he might be seen to be life, by making his flesh live again.

(36) Come now, let the manner of our own death also be closely examined. No one at all in his right mind will say that our souls perish together with our bodies which are made of earth. Except for man, I think that this is not doubtful of other living beings. Except for man, death is called a natural concomitant. In this way, you will think also about Emmanuel himself. For he was the Word in flesh of his own, born of a woman, and he yielded it to death at the proper moment, suffering nothing himself in his own nature, for he is life and life-giver. He made his own the necessities of the flesh in order that the suffering may be said to be his also, and being the first of all who rose again after he had died for all, in order that he might pay for the human race with his own blood, and might win over for

---

79. Cf. Phil 2.7.   81. Rom 8.15.
80. Cf. Eph 3.17.   82. Heb 12.2.

God the Father all those who are in the whole world. That this is true the blessed prophet Isaiah proclaims, saying in the Spirit, "Therefore he himself shall inherit many, and he shall divide the spoils of the strong, because he has delivered his soul unto death and was reputed among the wicked; and he has borne the sins of many, and he was delivered for their iniquities."[83]

(37) One, therefore, more worthy than all others laid down his own life for all and yielded his flesh to be constrained briefly by death according to the divine plan. But as life, he has destroyed death in turn, not enduring to suffer contrary to his own nature, in order that corruption in the bodies of all might be weakened and the power of death undone. For as we all die in Adam, so also in Christ, we all shall be made to live. For if he had not suffered as man for our sake, neither would he have done as God the things which wrought our salvation. For it is said that he died as man first, but that he came back to life after that because he is God according to nature. If, therefore, he has not suffered death in his flesh according to the Scriptures, neither was he brought back to life in spirit, that is, he did not come to life again. And if this is true, our faith is vain and we are still in our sins. For we have been baptized into his death, according to the words of blessed Paul,[84] and we have obtained remission of our sins through his blood.

(38) But if, indeed, the Christ is neither truly the Son nor God by nature, but mere man as we are, and an instrument of divinity, we have not been saved by God, have we, but rather, since one like ourselves died for us and was raised up by the powers of someone else? How, then, was death still destroyed by Christ? And yet I hear him saying clearly concerning his own life, "No one takes it from me, but I lay it down of myself. I have the power to lay it down, and I have the power to take it up again."[85] For as one of us, though he knew not death, he went down into death through his own flesh in order that we might also go up with him to life. For he came to life again,

83. Is 53.12.
84. Rom 6.3, cf. 1 Pt 3.18, 1 Cor 15.17 and Eph 1.7.
85. Jn 10.18.

having despoiled the nether world, not as a man like us, but as God in flesh among us and above us. Our nature was greatly enriched with immortality in him first and death was crushed when it assaulted the body of life as an enemy. For just as it conquered in Adam, so it was defeated in Christ. And the inspired Psalmist dedicated songs of victory to him ascending on our account and in our behalf to God the Father in heaven, so that heaven might be seen to be accessible to those on earth, for he says, "God is ascended with jubilee, and the Lord with the sound of trumpet. Sing praises to our God, sing you; sing praises to our king, sing you, sing you wisely; for God has reigned over the nations."[86] And the blessed Paul spoke somewhere of him saying, "He who descended, he it is who ascended also above the heavens, that he might fill all things."[87]

(39) Because, therefore, he is truly God and king according to nature, and because the one crucified has been called the Lord of glory,[88] how could anyone hesitate to call the Holy Virgin the Mother of God? Adore him as one, without dividing him into two after the union. Then, the senseless Jew shall laugh in vain; then, in truth, he shall be the one who slew the Lord, and he shall be convicted as the one who has sinned, not against one of those who are like us, but against God himself, the Savior of all. And especially, he shall hear, "Ah! sinful nation, people full of sins! vile race! iniquitous children! you have utterly forsaken the Lord and you have provoked to wrath the holy one of Israel."[89] But the children of the gentiles in no way shall ridicule the faith of the Christians. For we have adored not a mere man, God forbid, but rather we, not ignorant of his glory, have adored him who is God according to nature, and even if he became like us, he has remained what he was, that is, God.

(40) Through him and with him may there be glory to God the Father, with the holy and life-giving Spirit, unto ages of ages. Amen.

86. Cf. Ps 46(47)6–9.
87. Cf. Eph 4.10.
88. Cf. 1 Cor 2.8.
89. Is 1.4. For Cyril's attitude towards the Jews see R. L. Wilken, *Judaism and the Early Christian Mind* (Yale University Press, 1971), 54–68.

LETTER 2

To his most pious and most God-loving fellow bishop Nestorius, Cyril sends greetings in the Lord.[1]

ENERABLE MEN WORTHY of belief have arrived in Alexandria. They reported that your reverence was both extremely annoyed and was leaving no stone unturned to vex me. When I wished to learn what your reverence's vexation was, they told me that some men from Alexandria are carrying around the letter sent to the holy monks and that this has been the origin of your dislike and displeasure. I am surprised if your reverence has not taken into account a well-known fact, for there was confusion about the faith not before the letter was written by me but before what was said, or left unsaid, by your reverence. Besides, when documents and even commentaries were being circulated, we were pained because we desire to correct those who have gone astray. For some have come close to refusing to confess any longer that Christ is God, but rather an instrument and a tool of divinity, and a man bearing God. What is further from the truth than such beliefs? Therefore, our irritation was at the things which your reverence had said, or had not said. For I do not greatly trust the documents being circulated. How, therefore, is it possible to be silent when the faith is being damaged and so many have been misled?

(2) Or shall we not stand before the tribunal of Christ? Shall we not defend ourselves against unseasonal silence, since we have been appointed by him to say what ought to be said? But what shall I do now? Since the most pious and most God-loving

1. For the critical text of this letter see Schwartz, *ACO* 1.1.1 pp. 23–25. Geerard numbers this letter 5302 in *CPG*. See also Festugière, *Éphèse*, 45–46.

Bishop of Rome, Celestine, and the most God-loving bishops with him denounced them, I must take counsel with your reverence concerning the documents which were brought here, I don't know how, as to whether at any time they are your reverence's or not. For the writers have been completely shocked. How shall we take care of those who come from all the churches of the East and murmur against the documents? Or perhaps your reverence thinks that little disturbance was produced in the churches in consequence of such communications. We are all in struggles and labors, bringing back to the truth those who have been persuaded, I do not know how, to think the opposite. When it is your reverence that inflicted on all the necessity of murmuring, how do you rightly censure me? Why do you cry out against me without reason? And might you not rather amend your utterance in order that a worldwide scandal might stop? For even if an utterance has escaped your lips, passing, so to speak, from mouth to mouth among the people, yet let it be corrected by study and deign to furnish a statement for those being scandalized, by you yourself calling the Holy Virgin the Mother of God, in order that by taking care of those saddened and by having sound doctrine in the eyes of all, we may bring it to pass that the people assemble in peace and unity of spirit.

(3) But do not let your reverence doubt that we are ready to suffer all things for the sake of the faith in Christ, both the trial of imprisonment and death itself. In fact, I say that, while Atticus[2] of happy memory still lived, a book concerning the holy and consubstantial Trinity was composed by me in which also is a treatise about the Incarnation of the only begotten in

2. Atticus was Patriarch of Constantinople from 406 to 425. He and another priest, Arsacius, were the chief accusers of St. John Chrysostom at the Synod of the Oak in 403 which deposed him on false charges, with the assistance of Theophilus, Patriarch of Alexandria, uncle of Cyril, who presided. Chrysostom never was reinstated. Arsacius, already an old man, was appointed to his place without Rome's approval. When he died in 405, Atticus was appointed. Pope Innocent I had broken off communion with the Patriarchs of Alexandria, Antioch, and Constantinople, and this state of affairs lasted until 407, when Chrysostom died. Atticus reformed afterwards, and was praised by Celestine I for fighting against the Pelagians.

harmony with which I have now written. I read it to him, to bishops, to clerics, and to those of the faithful who listened eagerly. Thus far, I have given a copy to no one. It is likely that when that treatise is published I will be accused again, because, even before the election of your reverence, the little treatise was composed.

LETTER 3

To my most God-loving and most holy fellow bishop, Cyril, Nestorius sends greetings in the Lord.[1]

NOTHING IS MORE forceful than Christian forbearance. By it now, through that most pious priest, Lampon, we have been constrained to write this letter, for he said much to us about your piety and heard much. In the end, he did not yield until he exacted the letter from us and we have been conquered by the forcefulness of the man. For I confess that I have great respect for all the Christian forbearance of every man since it possesses God indwelling in it. As far as we are concerned, even though many things have been done by your reverence not in keeping with fraternal love, for it is necessary to speak rather mildly, we write with largeness of heart and love in salutation. Experience will show what sort of fruit there is for us of the violence from the most esteemed priest, Lampon.

(2) We and those with us greet you with all brotherly affection.

1. For the critical text of this letter see Schwartz, *ACO* 1.1.1 p. 25. Geerard numbers this letter 5303 in *CPG*. See also Festugière, *Éphèse*, 47.

LETTER 4

To his most pious and God-loving bishop, Nestorius, Cyril sends greetings in the Lord.[1]

OME MEN KEEP on chattering, as I hear, of my reply to your reverence, and do this often, especially watching out for the assemblies of the magistrates. Perhaps because they think they are tickling your ears, they utter ill-advised words too. They do so even though they have not been wronged but duly convicted: one of being unjust to the blind and the poor, another of brandishing a sword at his mother, another of stealing someone else's money with the help of a maid servant. They have had an enduring reputation so bad that one would not wish it upon his worst enemies. However, let there be no lengthy accounts by me of such matters in order that I may not extend the measure of my self-importance beyond my Lord and teacher[2] nor, indeed, beyond the Fathers. For it is not possible to escape the perversities of evil men, however one may choose to pass his life.

(2) But they, with mouth full of curses and bitterness, will defend themselves before the judge of all. I shall now turn myself again to what most becomes me, and I shall remind you now, as a brother in Christ, that you should preach doctrine to the laity and a tenet of the faith with all caution. You should consider that scandalizing even only one of the little ones believing in Christ[3] has an unendurable punishment. If the

1. For the critical text of this letter see Schwartz, *ACO* 1.1.1 pp. 25–28 or *ACO* 2.1.1 pp. 104–106. Geerard numbers this letter 5304 in *CPG*. See also Festugière, *Éphèse*, 48–51, and L. R. Wickham, *Cyril of Alexandria: Select Letters* (Oxford, 1983), 2–11.

2. Cf. Jn 13.13 and 2 Pt 2.1.

3. Cf. Mt 18.6.

number of those harmed be so great, do we not stand in need of all skill to remove the scandals prudently and explain the sound teaching of the faith to those seeking the truth? If we abide by the teachings of the holy Fathers and are earnest in considering them of great value, and test ourselves, "whether we are in the faith"[4] according to the Scripture, it will truly come about that we most fitly will mold our thoughts to their upright and blameless judgments.

(3) Accordingly, the holy and great council[5] said that the only begotten Son himself, begotten of God the Father according to his nature, true God of true God, light of light, he through whom the Father made all things, descended, was made flesh and became man, suffered, rose on the third day and ascended into heaven. We must follow these words and teachings, keeping in mind what having been made flesh means; and that it makes clear that the Logos from God became man. We do not say that the nature of the Word was altered when he became flesh. Neither do we say that the Word was changed into a complete man of soul and body. We say rather that the Word by having united to himself hypostatically flesh animated by a rational soul, inexplicably and incomprehensibly became man. He has been called the Son of man, not according to desire alone or goodwill, nor by the assumption of a person only. We say that, although the natures are different which were brought together to a true unity, there is one Christ and Son from both. The differences of the natures are not destroyed through the union, but rather the divinity and humanity formed for us one Lord Jesus Christ and one Son through the incomprehensible and ineffable combination to a unity.

(4) Thus, although he had existence before the ages and was begotten of the Father, he is said to have been begotten also according to the flesh from a woman. His divine nature did not take a beginning of existence in the Holy Virgin, nor did his divine nature need another begetting of necessity for its

4. Cf. 2 Cor 13.5.
5. i.e., of Nicaea.

own sake after being begotten of the Father. For it is purpose-less, and at the same time also stupid, to say that he who exists before all ages and is coeternal with the Father needs a second beginning for existence. But since for our sake and for our salvation he united a human nature to himself hypostatically and was born from a woman, in this manner, he is said to have been born according to the flesh. For an ordinary man was not born of the Holy Virgin and then the Word descended into him, but, united with flesh in her womb, the Word is said to have endured birth according to the flesh, so as to claim as his own the birth of his own flesh.

(5) Thus we say that he also suffered and rose again, not that the Word of God suffered in his own nature, or received blows, or was pierced, or received the other wounds, for the divine cannot suffer since it is incorporeal. But since his own body, which had been born, suffered these things, he himself is said to have suffered them for our sake. For he was the one, incapable of suffering, in the body which suffered. In the same fashion, we also think of his death. For the Word of God is immortal by nature and incorruptible, being both life and life-giving. But because by the grace of God his own body tasted death for all, as Paul says,[6] he himself is said to have suffered death for our sake. As far as the nature of the Word was concerned, he did not experience death, for it would be madness to say or think that, but, as I said, his flesh tasted death. This, too, when his flesh was resuscitated, it is again called his Resurrection; not as if he fell into corruption, God forbid, but that his body rose again.

(6) Thus we will confess one Christ and Lord, not that we worship a man together with the Word in order that an appearance of division may not be introduced by saying *with*. But we adore one and the same Lord since his body is not foreign to the Word, in union with which he sits by his Father's side.[7] We do not state that two sons sit beside the Father, but that one does through unity with his own flesh. But if we reject

---

6. Cf. Heb 2.9.

7. Here there is a variation in the texts printed in *ACO* 1.1.1 p. 28 and *ACO* 2.1.1 p. 106. The former reads αὐτῷ, while the latter reads αὐτός. The effect of

the hypostatic unity as either unattainable or improper, we fall into saying that there are two sons. For there is every necessity of distinguishing and of saying that he, as a man considered separately, was honored in a special manner by the appellation 'the Son', and again separately the Word of God in a special manner possesses by nature both the name and the reality of filiation. Therefore, the one Lord Jesus Christ is not to be divided into two sons.

(7) In no way will it be profitable that the true account of the faith mean this even if some admit the union of persons. For the Scripture has not said that the Word united the person of a man to himself, but that he became flesh.[8] The Word becoming flesh is nothing else except that he partook of blood and flesh just as we are. He made our flesh his own, and was born man from a woman without having thrown aside his divinity and his being begotten of God the Father, but, in the assumption of flesh, he remained what he was. The doctrine of the precise faith everywhere maintains this. We shall find that the holy Fathers have thought in this way. In this way, they have not hesitated to call the Holy Virgin the Mother of God. They do not say that the nature of the Word or his divinity took the beginning of being from the Holy Virgin, but that his holy body, animated by a rational soul, was born of her, united to which [soul and body] in actual fact the Word is said to have been begotten according to the flesh.[9] And I write these things now from love in Christ, exhorting you as a brother, and calling you to witness in the presence of Christ and his chosen angels that you think and teach these doctrines with us, in order that the peace of the churches may be saved and the bond of concord and love between the priests of God may continue unbroken.[10]

αὐτῷ is to stress that he [Christ] sits by *his Father's* side, while the effect of αὐτός is to stress that *he* [Christ] sits by his Father's side.

8. Cf. Jn 1.14.

9. Cyril's orthodoxy was well known before the controversy with Nestorius. See J. Liébaert, *La doctrine christologique de saint Cyrille d'Alexandrie avant la querelle Nestorienne* (Lille, 1951), 197–217.

10. The text of Letter 4 in *ACO* 2.1.1 p. 106 ends at this point. The two sentences that follow are only included in Schwartz's edition of Letter 4 in *ACO* 1.1.1 p. 28.

(8) Salute the brotherhood with you. The brotherhood with us greets you in Christ.[11]

11. Letter 4 has been called the *epistula dogmatica*. It was approved unanimously at the first meeting of the Council of Ephesus, June 22, 431. Pope Leo the Great approved it in 450 as did the Councils of Chalcedon in 451 and Constantinople in 553. See Quasten 3.133.

LETTER 5

To his most pious and God-loving fellow bishop, Cyril, Nestorius sends greetings in the Lord.[1]

DISMISS THE OUTRAGES against me of your amazing letters as deserving healing forbearance and of being answered in due season through circumstances themselves. But as to that which does not permit of silence, since it involves great danger if silence be kept, of this, as far as I may be able, I shall attempt to make a concise statement without exerting myself to wordiness, being on my guard against the nausea of obscure and indigestible tediousness. I shall begin from the very wise utterances of your charity, citing them in your very words. Which, therefore, are the utterances of the amazing teaching of your letters?

(2) The holy and great council says that he, the only begotten Son, was begotten by nature of God the Father, true God of true God, light of light, through whom the Father made all things, that he descended, was made flesh and became man, suffered and rose. These are the words of your reverence, and perhaps you recognize your own.

(3) But hear also our words, a brotherly exhortation to piety, and that which the great Paul solemnly stated to his beloved Timothy, "Be diligent in reading, in exhortation, and in teaching. For in so doing you will save both yourself and those who hear you."[2] What, pray tell, does "be diligent" imply? It means that in reading the teaching of those holy Fathers without due attention you failed to recognize a pardonable

---

1. For the critical text of this letter see Schwartz, *ACO* 1.1.1 pp. 29–32. Geerard numbers this letter 5305 in *CPG*. See also Festugière, *Éphèse,* 52–56.
2. 1Tm 4.13, 16.

misconception. You thought that they had said that the Word, who is coeternal with the Father, is able to suffer.[3] Look closely, if you please, at the precise meaning of their words, and you will find that the inspired chorus of the Fathers has not said that the consubstantial divinity is able to suffer, nor that divinity, coeternal with the Father, was begotten, nor that divinity rose from the dead when raising his destroyed temple. If you give ear to brotherly correction, by citing for you the very utterances, I shall rid you of your misinterpretation of those holy Fathers, and through them of the inspired Scriptures.

(4) I believe, therefore, in our Lord Jesus Christ, his only begotten Son. Notice how they place first as foundations the words, Lord, Jesus, Christ, only begotten, and Son, the words common to divinity and humanity. Then they build upon it the tradition of the Incarnation, the Resurrection, and the Passion. They do so once the terminology signifying what is common to both natures has been presented, so that what belongs to filiation and lordship may not be separated, and what belongs to the natures be in no danger of confusion in the oneness of filiation.

(5) For in this Paul himself has been their teacher. When mentioning the divine Incarnation and about to go on to the Passion, he uses first the name Christ, a name common to both natures, as I said a short time earlier, and then he adds a specific term. What are his words? "Have this mind in you which was also in Christ Jesus, for though being in the form of God, he did not consider being equal to God a thing to be clung to, but (to omit details) became obedient to death, even to death on a cross."[4] When he was about to mention his death, in order that no one might assume from this that God the Word was subject to suffering, he puts the word Christ first as a name signifying the substance capable of suffering and of the nature incapable of suffering in one person, so that without danger Christ may be called incapable and capable of suffering, incapable because of his divinity and capable because of the nature

3. Cyril did not say this, cf. Letter 4.
4. Phil 2.5–8.

of his body. I could say much about this and, as said earlier,
that the holy Fathers mentioned not a begetting according to
the 'economy', but an incarnation, but I perceive that the
promise of brevity in my exordium curbs my speech and calls
forth the second topic of your charity.

(6) In it, I praise the distinction of the natures according to
the definition of humanity and divinity, and the conjunction of
them into one person, and not saying that God the Word had
need of a second begetting from a woman, and the profession
that the divinity does not admit of suffering. In truth such
doctrines are orthodox and opposite to the infamous opinions
of all heresies concerning the natures of the Lord. But if the
rest bring on some arcane wisdom incomprehensible for your
audience to understand, it is for you to scrutinize. To me, at
least, they seem to overthrow the first, for they introduced, I
do not know how, him who was proclaimed in the first statements as incapable of suffering and not capable of receiving a
second begetting, as, in turn, capable of suffering and newly
created. This is as if the properties belonging to God the Word
according to nature were destroyed by the union with his
temple; or as if it is considered of little import to men that the
temple, which is without flaw and inseparable from the divine
nature, for the sake of sinners endured both birth and death;
or as if the voice of the Lord ought not to be believed when
saying to the Jews, "Destroy this temple, and in three days I
shall raise it up."[5] He did not say, "Destroy my divinity, and in
three days I will raise it up." Although I would like to amplify
my statements, I am restrained by recalling my promise.
Nevertheless, this has to be said, though I am observing
brevity.

(7) Everywhere in Sacred Scripture whenever it makes
mention of the 'economy' of the Lord, the birth for our sake
and the Passion are ascribed, not to the divinity, but to the
humanity of Christ. So according to the most precise appellation, the Holy Virgin is called the Mother of Christ, not the
Mother of God. Listen to these words of the Gospels that say,

5. Jn 2.19.

"The book of the generation of Jesus Christ, the son of David, the son of Abraham."[6] It is plain that God the Word was not the son of David. Accept another testimony, if you please, "Jacob begot Joseph, the husband of Mary, and of her was born Jesus who is called Christ."[7] Notice yet another voice testifying for us, "Now the origin of Christ was in this wise. When Mary his mother had been betrothed to Joseph, she was found to be with child by the Holy Spirit."[8] Whoever would assume that the divinity of the only begotten was a creation of the Holy Spirit? What need to say, "The mother of Jesus was there"[9] and again, "with Mary the Mother of Jesus"[10] and, "that which is begotten in her is of the Holy Spirit"[11] and, "take the child and his mother and flee into Egypt"[12] and, "concerning his Son who was born according to the flesh of the offspring of David"?[13] And again concerning his Passion, "Since God sent his Son in the likeness of sinful flesh, and concerning sin he has condemned sin in the flesh"[14] and again, "Christ died for our sins"[15] and, "since Christ suffered in the flesh"[16] and, "This is (not my divinity, but) my body, which is broken for you."[17] And heed the countless other voices testifying to the human race that they should not think that the divinity of the Son was recent, or capable of receiving bodily suffering, but that the flesh was, which was joined to the nature of the divinity. Wherefore, also, Christ calls himself both David's Lord and Son, for he says, "What do you think of the Christ? Whose son is he?" They say to him, "David's." Jesus answered and said to them, "How then does David in the Spirit call him Lord saying, 'The Lord said to my Lord, sit at my right hand,'"[18] as he is the Son of David by all means according to the flesh, but his Lord according to his divinity.

(8) Therefore, it is right and worthy of the Gospel traditions

6. Mt 1.1.
7. Mt 1.16.
8. Mt. 1.18.
9. Jn 2.1.
10. Cf. Acts 1.14.
11. Cf. Mt 1.20.
12. Mt. 2.13.
13. Rom 1.3.
14. Cf. Rom 8.3.
15. 1 Cor 15.3.
16. Cf. 1 Pt 4.1.
17. Cf. Lk 22.19 and 1 Cor 11.24.
18. Cf. Mt 22.42–44.

to confess that the body is the temple of the Son's divinity and a temple joined to the divinity according to a certain sublime and divine union, and that his divine nature makes his own the things of his body. But in the name of this relationship to attribute also to his divinity the properties of the united flesh, I mean birth, suffering, and death, is, my brother, the act of a mind truly led astray like the pagans or diseased like the minds of that mad Apollinaris, Arius, and the other heresies, but rather more grievously than they. For it is necessary that such as are dragged into error by the word relationship make the Word God partake of the nourishment of milk through the relationship, and have a share in growing, little by little,[19] and of fear at the time of his Passion,[20] and be in need of angelic assistance.[21] And I pass over in silence that circumcision, sacrificing, sweat, hunger, and thirst, which happened to his body on account of us, are worshipfully united to the divinity. If these are taken with reference to the divinity, and falsely, there is a cause for just condemnation against us as slanderers.

(9) These are the teachings handed down by the holy Fathers; these are the precepts of the Holy Scriptures. Thus one teaches about God the actions of the divine benevolence and majesty. "Meditate on these things, give yourself entirely to them, that your progress may be manifest to all, and towards all,"[22] as Paul says.

(10) But you do well to cling to your anxiety for those scandalized, and I give thanks that your spirit, anxious over things divine, took thought of our affairs. But realize that you have been led astray by those condemned by the holy synod[23] as Manichean sympathizers of the clerics who perhaps share your opinions. For the affairs of the church daily go forward, and the numbers of the faithful are so increasing through the grace of God that those who behold the multitudes of them repeat

19. Cf. Lk 2.52.
20. Cf. Mt 26.38–45; Mk 14.33–41; Lk 22.39–46.
21. Cf. Lk 22.43.
22. 1 Tm 4.15.
23. This is a reference to the condemnation of Philip, a presbyter of the Church of Constantinople. Reference is again made to Philip in the Memorandum sent by Cyril to Pope Celestine. See Letter 11(a).

the words of the prophet, "The earth will be filled with the knowledge of the Lord, as much water would veil the seas,"[24] since the teaching has shed its light upon the interests of the emperor, and, to put it briefly, one would very joyfully find fulfilled day by day among us the famous saying with regard to all the ungodly heresies and the correct teaching of the church, "The house of Saul went forth and grew weak. And the house of David went forth and was strengthened."[25] These are our counsels, as of a brother to a brother. "But if anyone is disposed to be contentious," as Paul shall cry out against such a one through us, "we have no such custom, neither have the churches of God."[26]

(11) I and those with me greet especially all the brotherhood with you. May you continue to be vigorous in Christ and pray for us, my most God-loving friend who is dear to me in every way.

24. Cf. Is 11.9.
25. Cf. 2 Sm (2 Kgs) 3.1. The first part indicates a protracted war between the house of Saul and the house of David.
26. 1 Cor 11.16.

LETTERS 6 and 7

To my brother and fellow bishop.[1]

 DID NOT BELIEVE that what was said about you heretofore was true; nor did I think that the letter, which was delivered to me under your name, was written by you, since in it I found the most false opinions full of blasphemy attributed to the saints. Therefore, I advise you to desist from such blasphemies and contentions. You do not have such strength that you are able to fight against God, who truly was crucified for us and died in the flesh, and lives through the power of his divinity, "He it is who sits at the right hand of the Father,[2] and angels, principalities, and powers adore him,[3] and he is the eternal king into whose hands the Father has given all things."[4] He himself is the creator of all against whom you are unable either to rise up or struggle.

(2) Nor is there need that I recall to your memory what

---

1. Geerard 5306 in *CPG* includes the text of two letters from Cyril to Nestorius which Eusèbe Renaudot had numbered Letters 6 and 7 in his *Historia Jacobitarum Patriarcharum Alexandrinorum* (Paris, 1713). Renaudot's edition of Letters 6 and 7, reproduced in PG 77.57–60 is in substantial agreement with the critical Arabic text published by B. Evetts, *History of the Patriarchs of the Coptic Church of Alexandria* (Arabic text edited, translated, and annotated) PO 1:433–436. The Arabic text adds further Scripture references: Mk 14.61, 62; 1 Tm 6.13; Lk 1.32–35; Phil 2.6-7; 1 Thes 1.10; Heb 1.4–6; and Heb 2.5, 8–9 and concludes with these words: "You now see this wisdom full of faith in our Lord Jesus Christ. I have sent you these letters, my brother, that you may keep them in the church. You are not without knowledge, so read the Scriptures and learn this and more from them. I have sent brothers to you and asked them to remain with you that you may inquire diligently for a month and search the Scriptures and inform us of the results. Farewell." The letters are together in Arabic.
2. Cf. Ps 109(110).1; Heb 1.13.
3. Cf. Heb 1.6.
4. Cf. 1 Cor 15.26.

happened to the Jews, his enemies, since they are sufficiently well known to you, or the things which happened to the heretics, Simon Magus, Julian the emperor, and Arius. Behold, Job the just man says, "See my affliction, and fear and praise the Lord."[5] I declare to you that the church is not going to permit your shamelessness against her God, and she is the very church against whom the gates of hell have not been able to prevail.[6] You yourself know how many trials she has endured, in such a way, however, that no one has prevailed against her because she is as a rock in her faith. Look, therefore, at what you are about to do, and farewell.[7]

(3) If you were not a bishop, no one except your friends and relatives would have recognized you. Now, however, because you sit upon the episcopal throne of the Son of God, everyone recognizes you because of the dignity of the church over which you preside. However, you are attacking the Lord through words of blasphemy which you are able neither to explain nor prove. Although you may examine the Old Testament you will not find Christ called a mere man in it, as you suppose. Further, you seem to suppose you are able to resist God, your creator, who redeemed you with his blood, who is God, the Son of God the Father, as he is called in the Old and New Testaments, and who, in the Gospel of John, is called, "the only begotten Son who is in the bosom of the Father."[8] Matthew the Evangelist also says that he is "Emmanuel which is interpreted God with us,"[9] as Isaiah had said in his prophesy.[10]

5. Cf. Jn 6.21.
6. Cf. Mt 16.18.
7. Nestorius replied arrogantly to this letter and in his answer favored blasphemies similar to the earlier ones. Cyril answered him sharply in Letter 7.
8. Jn 1.18.
9. Mt 1.23.
10. Cf. Is 7.14.

LETTER 8

A letter of Cyril against those who accused him in writing that he did not maintain silence on hearing that the impious teaching of Nestorius was making more menacing inroads.[1]

INCE YOUR PIETY has written to me that the most devout Nestorius was grieved because of the letter I wrote to the monks desiring to hold in check those who were scandalized at the rumor, I say this of necessity, that it arose not so much from us as from his reverence. I expounded the doctrine of the true faith to those scandalized by his interpretations. He himself in the Catholic and Orthodox Church allowed the good bishop, Dorotheus,[2] openly to say, "If anyone says that Mary is the Mother of God, let him be anathema." And when he heard this, he was not only silent when Dorotheus spoke, but admitted him immediately into mystical communion and made him his fellow communicant.

(2) See, therefore, that we have been anathematized in his very presence, not to say by him, with him presiding, for Dorotheus would not have spoken such things in the church against the will of Nestorius. Now both we the living, the bishops throughout the world, and our Fathers who have gone to God have been anathematized. What then hindered us also from writing the opposite to his words and saying, "If anyone does not call Mary the Mother of God, let him be anathema"? But I have not done this so far because of him, in order that

1. For the critical text of this letter see Schwartz, *ACO* 1.1.1 p. 109. Geerard numbers this letter 5307 in *CPG*. See also Festugière, *Éphèse*, 163–164.

2. Dorotheus was Bishop of Marcianopolis, a see in Lower Moesia on the right bank of the Danube, named after Trajan's sister, Marciana. At the time of the Council of Ephesus he sided with the group around John of Antioch, and signed the act which deposed Cyril and Memnon, Bishop of Ephesus.

some may not say that the Bishop of Alexandria or the Egyptian synod anathematized him. If the most devout bishops throughout the East and West should learn that they were all anathematized, (for all say and confess that holy Mary is the Mother of God), how will they be disposed? Or how will not all be grieved, if not for their own sakes, at all events for the holy Fathers, in whose writings we always find the Holy Virgin Mary named Mother of God? If the result had not seemed to be a burdensome thing, I would have sent you many books of many of the holy Fathers in which it is possible to find, not once, but very often, the customary expression by which they confess the Holy Virgin Mary to be the Mother of God.

LETTER 9

A letter of Cyril to a certain devotee of Nestorius.[1]

KNOW THE SINCERITY of your charity and I have not been ignorant of your zeal. If I were writing to someone who did not know my character, I would have used many words persuading him that I am very peaceful, and not quarrelsome or warlike but, on the contrary, praying to love all and be loved by all. But since I am writing to one who knows me, I explain this concisely, that if it were possible to endure the loss of possessions or money, and to put an end to grief for a brother, I would gladly have done so, in order not to appear to consider anything more honorable than love. But when it is a matter of faith, and all the churches throughout the Roman Empire, so to speak, have been scandalized, what are we to do? For there is no one, from whatever city or land he may come, who does not say, "What are these rumors" and "What kind of new doctrine is attacking the churches?" What shall we do against these evils, we who have been entrusted by God with the doctrine of the mystery, against whom on the day of judgment those who are introduced into the mysteries will certainly testify? For they will say that they kept the faith as they were introduced to it by us. And if we have done this rightly, we shall both receive a reward and meet with praise, but if we do otherwise and perversely, what kind of flames will be enough to punish us? For we shall hear, "You destroyed my land and you killed my people,"[2] according to the Scripture. Each of those who are laymen in rank will give an account of his own

1. For the critical text of this letter see Schwartz, *ACO* 1.1.1 p. 108. Geerard numbers this letter 5308 in *CPG*. See also Festugière, *Éphèse*, 161–162.
2. Is 14.20.

53

life. But we who have been heavily laden with the duties of the episcopacy will give an account, not only of ourselves, but of all those believing in Christ.

(2) For me, then, there is no consideration of pain or of insolence or of the amount of abuse which some disreputable men have hurled against me. But let all this depart into oblivion. God will also judge those who have blabbered nonsense. Only let the doctrines of the faith be safe and I am friendly and affectionate, and yield to no one in the obligation of showing greater love to the God-loving bishop, Nestorius. To speak before God, I wish him to be of good repute in Christ, to blot out the disgrace for what is already past, and to show that the gossip of some people against his faith is slander and not at all truth.

(3) But if we have been commanded by Christ to love even those who hate us,[3] how is it not more reasonable to do this for our brothers and fellow bishops? There is no doubt that, if the faith is lost by some, we will not abandon their souls, not even if suffering and death itself be before us. If we fear to speak the truth for the glory of God so that we might not fall into unpleasantness, with what countenance before the people shall we any longer recount the praises of the holy martyrs whom we honor because they have observed the saying, "unto death fight for truth"?[4]

3. Cf. Mt 5.44.
4. Cf. Sir 4.28.

LETTER 10

A letter[1] of the same.[2]

READ THE MEMORANDUM dispatched by you, through which I learned that when Anastasius the priest met you, he pretended to be seeking friendship and peace and said, "As he wrote to the monks; so we think." Then, looking toward his own objective, he said about me, "He himself also said that the holy council[3] did not mention the expression; I mean, Mother of God." But I had written that even if the council did not mention the expression, it had acted rightly, for at that time no such question had been raised. Wherefore it was not necessary to bring forward matters which were not being questioned, particularly if the synod recognized by the meaning of the terms the Holy Virgin to be the Mother of God. It said that he, the begotten of the Father, through whom all things were made, was incarnate, was made man, suffered, rose from the dead, ascended into heaven, and will come as judge of the living and of the dead. The council did not in any way say that the Word itself, begotten of God by nature, died or was pierced in the side by a spear. For what sort of side, pray tell, does that which is incorporeal have? Or how could life die? But the council said that, because the Word was united to flesh, when his flesh was suffering he appropriated the suffering to himself since his own body was suffering. Therefore, they who say such things are deceiving and beguiling themselves, be-

---

1. For the critical text of this letter see Schwartz, *ACO* 1.1.1 pp. 110–112. Geerard numbers this letter 5309 in *CPG*.
2. From St. Cyril, Bishop of Alexandria, to the clergy in Constantinople.
3. Nicaea.

55

cause they are mistaken and have their own poison in their hearts.

(2) It is possible to see this from the following. Two documents were dispatched to Bupha Martyr, the deacon, in whose care are ecclesiastical matters. One document was put together by Photius, or by someone else, against the work which I sent to the monks. The other, in the form of a pamphlet, had an outrageous title which read as follows: "Addressed to those who, because of the combination, either minimize the divinity of the only begotten or deify his humanity." The introduction is directed against the insults of heretics as springing from obstinacy, and then attempts to show that it was his body that suffered and not God the Word, as if some say that the Word of God, which is not capable of suffering, is capable of suffering. But no one is so mad.

(3) As we often said, the holy council said that the Word himself, through whom all things were made, suffered; but suffered in his flesh, according to the Scriptures. For, because his body suffered, he himself is said to have suffered, just as also a man's soul is said to suffer because its body suffers, although by its own nature the soul does not have pain. But since it is their aim to say that there are two christs and two sons, one being properly man, the other properly God, they then make the union be of persons only and, for this reason, they make subtle distinctions and weave "excuses in sin" as it is written.[4]

(4) Therefore, when you meet them, speak as follows, "You are wrong in inciting some to talk nonsense against your bishop, inflaming them and applauding them, and making them the instruments of their own wickedness. However, this is not the pretext for the distress, nor is your bishop entirely hostile to the bishop here. The fact that the teaching about Christ is not correct but distorted grieves all the bishops throughout the East and West."

(5) Sufficient proof and refutation are found in the fact that no one in the churches ever uttered such teachings as are

4. Ps 140(141).4.

contained in his explanations. Thus speaks Nestorius, "I judge your affection toward me not by outcry, but by your desire to be instructed and to be reminded of the divinity together with the humanity of the Lord." And a little later, "And I take heed that our people have much piety and the warmest reverence, but are incapacitated by the ignorance of divine mysteries. But this is not an accusation of the laity; rather, to speak becomingly, it is because their teachers do not have the opportunity to place before you some of the dogmas more precisely."[5]

(6) How could I put it properly? Did not those before him have leisure? Is he not more eloquent than John? Is he equal to or wiser than the blessed Atticus? What arrogance is this? But rather, how did he not distinctly confess that he introduced a strange and unfamiliar doctrine, and, through its absurdity, one not known to those before him, neither in the assembly of the faithful nor in the holy churches? There has been so far no discussion at all on my part against him concerning the matter. But rather it may happen that he repent and confess the true faith, and he will answer to God for the things which he has done to me in anger and by arousing enemies against me.

(7) It is no wonder if the offal of the city, Chaeremon, Victor, Sophronas, and the underling of fraudulent Flavian speak ill of me. They have already been a bad influence, both on one another and on everyone else. But let the one who incited them know that we fear neither death nor a defense in court against them, if there be an opportunity for this. It happens that the 'economy' of the Savior gathers a synod because of small and very slight matters in order to purify his church who keeps the true faith stainless and unconfused. Let the wretched man not think, even though there may be many reputable men who are likely to accuse us through regard for him, that he will be judge of our doctrines, even if this be introduced at court from ambition. When we have gone thither, we will challenge him and, God help us, he will defend his blasphemies. Hence in no way do we flee from peace, but rather grasp it, if the true faith be confessed and they cease

5. See Loofs, *Nestoriana*, 282.19–21 and 283.2–8.

saying these things; for by using their strange terminology they are calling death upon themselves. For the pamphlet which was sent has so many of his blasphemous distortions in it as to defile even the reader.

(8) But since it has charged that Scripture, or rather the holy council, has used an unaccustomed word when naming the Holy Virgin the Mother of God, let them be asked where is there evidence for *Christotokos* (Mother of Christ) or *Theodochos* (receptacle of God)? In addition, not knowing what he says, he inserted the following which is word for word, "Let us not make the Virgin, who was the receptacle of God, equal to God." For if she did not give birth to God, neither did she have Christ, who is God, in her womb, and how is she still the receptacle of God? And yet he calls God the Father God-begetting.[6] Where he reads these terms, I do not know. However, since many other matters for complaint drawn from his statements are slurred over, they will be kept safe until the right moment, unless some change of mind should take place.

(9) I received and read the rough draft of the petition which was sent by you as one which ought to be delivered to the emperor with our opinion. Since it contained much invective against the one there, or, should I say, my brother, I have withheld it so far, in order that he might not come forward against us saying, "You denounced me to the emperor as a heretic." We suggested otherwise, with also an appeal for his decision, stating the nature of his enmity and saying that the action should be shifted to other authorities if they completely resist.

(10) Accordingly, after reading the draft, deliver it, and, should need call for it, that is, if you see that he continues plotting and truly meddles in every way that deals with us, write to me quickly. And I have chosen discreet and prudent men, both bishops and monks, whom I shall send at the first opportunity. For "I will not grant sleep to my eyes, nor slumber to my eyelids, nor rest to my temples,"[7] according to the Scrip-

---

6. Nestorius applied to God the Father the term Θεοτόκος, which is normally applied to the Holy Virgin.

7. Cf. Ps 131(132).4, 5. Cf. also 1 Tm 6.12 and 2 Tm 4.7.

ture, until I have fought the fight for the salvation of all. Wherefore, having learned our opinions, act manfully. Presently there will be the necessary letters to the proper people.

(11) It is my aim for the faith in Christ to labor and endure any suffering whatsoever, no matter how terrible it is deemed to be, until I submit to death, which will be sweet to me because of this trouble.

LETTER 11

To his most holy and God-loving Father, Celestine, Cyril sends greetings in the Lord.[1]

F IT WERE POSSIBLE, by not writing to your reverence[2] everything going on, to be silent and without blame, and to escape appearing troublesome, especially in matters so necessary when even the truth of the faith is being undermined by some, I would have said to myself that silence is good and without danger, and to be at rest is better than to be involved in turmoil. But since God also demands of us wariness in these matters, and the long-standing customs of the churches persuade me to communicate with your holiness, I write of necessity revealing this, that satan is even now turning everything topsy-turvy, and rages against the churches of God, and tries to pervert the people everywhere who are walking uprightly in the faith. For that thoroughly depraved beast, productive of impiety, is not quiet.

(2) Accordingly I was silent during the time past, and I have written absolutely nothing either to your reverence concerning the one who is now in Constantinople and administers the church, nor have I written to any other of our fellow bishops, believing that in these matters precipitate action is not without blame. But since we have come to a crest of the evil, as it were, I thought it was absolutely necessary to loosen my tongue hereafter and to say that everything is in turmoil.

(3) For as soon as he was mentioned in the diptychs and consecrated it was necessary by exhortations toward good that

---

1. For the critical text of this letter see Schwartz, *ACO* 1.1.5 pp. 10–12. Geerard numbers this letter 5310 in *CPG*. See also Festugière, *Éphèse*, 528–531.
2. Celestine I, Pope, 422–432.

he help the people and the foreigners residing there, for these were very many and, as it were, from every city and land. But he made haste to say some extraordinary things quite beyond understanding, and such as are far from the faith of the apostles and the Gospels which the Fathers have protected above all and transmitted to us as a precious pearl. And I have sent to your reverence, as accurate evidence, the homilies which he gave in the church, and that frequently, and he does not cease to give them. I confess that, although I wished to make it clear to him by a synodical letter that we are unable to have dealings with one who says and thinks these things, I have not done this. But because I thought that it is necessary to offer a hand to those who slipped and to raise them as fallen brethren, I advised him through letters to desist from such false teachings. But we profited nothing. Since he has learned that we have recoiled so much from sharing his opinions as even to rebuke him to change his own particular novelties, for I would not say his teachings, he has set in motion every kind of plot, and still does not cease from causing disturbance. While we suppose him to be mending his ways and desisting from teachings against Christ, we learned from the following incident that we fell utterly short of our expectations.

(4) There was in Constantinople a bishop, Dorotheus[3] by name, who had the same opinions as he, a man easily flattered and froward of mouth, as is written.[4] When the most pious Nestorius was sitting on the throne in the assembly of the Church of Constantinople, he arose and dared to say in a loud voice, "If anyone says that Mary is the Mother of God, let him be anathema." And there was a great shout from all the people and they ran out. They did not want to associate any longer with those who had such opinions, so that even now the people of Constantinople keep away except from a few shallower ones, and those who flatter him. But nearly all the monasteries and their archimandrites, and many of the senators do not join him. They fear lest they be injured in faith, while he and those

3. Cf. Letter 8 note 2.
4. Cf. Prv 4.24, 13.3.

with him, whom he brought when going up from Antioch, say everything perverted.

(5) But after his homilies were brought to Egypt, I learned that some less sophisticated ones were misled, and then wavering were saying to one another, "Is he speaking the truth rightly? He has been led astray." Because I feared lest the teachings of the disease might strike roots in the souls of the more simple ones, I wrote a general letter to the monasteries in Egypt strengthening them in the true faith. Then some took copies to Constantinople, and they helped the readers very much, so that very many of those in authority have written thanking me. But this only fed his grievance against me and he struggles as with an enemy having nothing else to censure than just that I do not bear to share his teachings. I even strengthened in many the faith which we received from the Fathers, persuading them also to consider acceptable those things which we learned from Holy Scripture. Yet I do not consider the things done by him against me, but consign that to God, omniscient and almighty. I have written another letter to the person mentioned[5] containing as in a summary the exposition of the true faith, and at the same time exhorting and solemnly protesting that he should think and speak in the same manner. But again I profited nothing. He clings even until now to his original errors, and does not cease saying distorted things.

(6) Let your reverence know this too, that the things I am saying are agreeable to all the bishops of the East. All are displeased and pained, and especially the most pious bishops of Macedonia. Although he knows this, he thinks that he is wiser than all, and alone knows the meaning of the divinely inspired Scripture and the mystery of Christ. And when all the orthodox bishops and laity throughout the whole world confess that Christ is God and that the Virgin who bore him is the Mother of God, how should he fail to be fully convinced that he alone was straying from the faith by denying this? But he is a supercilious man and because of his position of authority he thinks that by plotting against all he will persuade us and all

5. That is, Letter 4. Cyril means Nestorius.

others to agree with his teachings. What, therefore, shall we do? We neither convince him nor are able to stop him from such homilies, and those in Constantinople have been daily ruined, even though they are displeased and are receiving assistance from orthodox teachers. Our statement is not about ordinary matters, but neither is silence without risk. For if Christ is blasphemed, how shall we be silent, especially as Paul writes, "If I do this willingly, I have a reward. But if unwillingly, I am nevertheless entrusted with a dispensation"?[6] What shall we say on the day of judgment, we who have been entrusted with the stewardship of the Word and the safety of the faith, we who were silent against these?

(7) But we do not throw off communion with him openly, until we have communicated these matters to your reverence. Wherefore deign to specify what seems best, and whether it is necessary to be in communion with him sometimes, or to forbid henceforward openly because no one is in communion who thinks and teaches such things. It is necessary that the intention of your reverence in these matters become clear by a letter both to the most devout and most God-loving bishops in Macedonia and to all those in the East. For we shall give them, as they earnestly desire, the means of staying of one mind and one opinion, and of contending for the true faith which is being attacked.

(8) As far as the matter stands according to him, both our great, admired, and well-esteemed Fathers and we who still live were anathematized along with them because we said that the Holy Virgin is the Mother of God. Since he did not desire to do this with his own lips, he set up another, the aforementioned Dorotheus, and prepared this statement, while he was sitting and listening, and, having come down from the throne, he immediately took communion with him as he[7] performed the divine mysteries.

(9) So that your holiness would know clearly what are the things which he says and thinks, and what our blessed and

---

6. 1 Cor 9.17. Paul is speaking about preaching the Gospel.
7. Nestorius.

great Fathers said and thought, I issued documents containing excerpts from the principal statements. I caused them to be translated[8] as far as it was possible for men in Alexandria, and I have given to the beloved Posidonius the letters written by me, commanding him to bring them to your holiness.

---

8. Translated into Latin. This passage indicates a lack of knowledge of Greek at Rome in the early fifth century A.D. and a lack of knowledge of Latin in Alexandria.

LETTER 11(a)

A Memorandum[1] of the most holy bishop Cyril to Posidonius in Rome, sent by him on account of matters pertaining to Nestorius.[2]

HIS IS THE TENOR of the faith of Nestorius or rather his false opinions. He says that God the Word, because he knew beforehand that the one born of the Holy Virgin would be holy and great, chose him for this and provided that he be born of the Virgin without man, granted him the favor of being called by his names, so that he is called both Son, Lord and Christ and prepared him to die for us and raised him from the dead. Wherefore, even if the only begotten Word of God is said to become man, because God was always with him as with a holy man born of the Virgin, for this reason the Word is said to have become man. Just as God was with the prophets, so, he says, God was with him in a closer 'conjunction'.[3]

(2) Because of this he avoids everywhere saying the 'union',[4] but calls it 'conjunction', as if there is one from without, and as if God might say to Jesus, "Just as I was with Moses, so I shall be with you."[5] But concealing his impiety he says that God was with him from the womb.

(3) And according to this he does not say that he is true God, but that he is thus named by the good pleasure of God, and

---

1. For the critical text of this Memorandum see Schwartz, *ACO* 1.1.7 pp. 171–172. Geerard numbers this Memorandum 5311 in *CPG*. Lampe lists it as Letter 11(a) in *PGL*, xx.

2. Letter 11 and this Memorandum sent to Rome indicate that in Cyril's day doctrinal matters were referred to Rome for decision.

3. This term, συνάφεια, is Nestorian. It is used along with the word τέμπλον in reference to Christ's body. See Letter 5, and Lampe, *PGL* 1309, s.v., "συνάφεια."

4. Cyril's term, ἕνωσις.

5. Cf. Jos 1.5 and 3.7.

even if he was named Lord, so again he wishes him to be Lord because the Word of God granted to him the favor of being named thus also.

(4) And he says that when we say that the Son of God died for us and rose from the dead, that the man died and the man rose, and nothing of this has to do with the Word of God.

(5) And we confess that the Word of God is immortal and is life, but we believe that he was made flesh, that is, by uniting to himself the flesh with a rational soul, he suffered in his flesh according to the Scriptures and that, since his body suffered, he himself is said to have suffered, although by nature he is impassible; and when his body arose, for his flesh did not see corruption,[6] we say that he rose for our sake. But these do not meet with his approval, but he says that the suffering is the man's, and the Resurrection the man's, and the body set forth in the mysteries is the man's. But we believe that the flesh of the Word is capable of giving life, because of this, that it is the flesh and blood of the Word, which gives life to all.

(6) Nestorius does not tolerate the saying of these things. He caused Celestius[7] to publish polemical documents against Philip, the priest, who opposed him and was no longer willing to be in communion with him because of his heresy. In the pamphlets there was an accusation of Manichaeanism. Then the man was summoned to a council. And he came ready to defend himself because he took doctrinal formulation to be the issue. But when Celestius had nothing to show, he absented himself and did not return to the council.

(7) Not finding this a pretext, he turned to another. For he said, "For what reason did you hold a rival meeting for worship, and offer the sacrifice in a house?" And although almost every cleric said, "Each of us does this in a crisis and in need" he issued a decree of degradation against the man.

(8) There you have the documents containing the main points of the blasphemies of Nestorius.

6. Cf. Acts 2.31.

7. He is believed to be the same Celestius who was a disciple of Pelagius. It was customary for Pelagius to call Catholics Manichaeans. See *ODCC*[2] 1058, s.v., "Pelagianism."

LETTER 12

Celestine, to his beloved brother, Cyril.[1]

O US IN OUR SADNESS the documents sent through our son Posidonius, the deacon, from your holiness brought joy and we exchanged our sorrow for happiness. As we looked at and reflected upon what the one who is attempting to disturb the church in Constantinople with his distorted homilies said, our soul was overwhelmed with no little sorrow. We were tormented by the goadings of various doubts, pondering the way to aid the preservation of the faith. But as we turned our attention to the writings[2] of your fraternity, immediately there appeared to us a most ready cure through which the pestilential disease may be completely driven out by a wholesome remedy. I mean the outflow of the pure spring which flows from the message of your love by which all the slime of the turgidly flowing stream shall be cleansed, and to all is opened up a way to the proper understanding of our faith.

(2) Just as therefore we brand and blame him, so in the love of the Lord we embrace your holiness as if present in your own writings, seeing that we think one and the same about the Lord. And it is no wonder that the most provident bishop of the Lord fights in behalf of the love of the faith with such valor that he resists the extraordinary boldness of the adversaries

1. For the critical text of this letter see Schwartz, *ACO* 1.1.1 pp. 75–77. Geerard numbers this letter 5312 in *CPG*. See also Festugière, *Éphèse*, 112–114.
2. Not all of Cyril's writings are meant, but only those mentioned at the end of the preceding letter, including the Memorandum. Pope Celestine is not here approving the famous formula of Cyril or the term ἕνωσις φυσική of Cyril's third anathema, cf. Letter 17.

and strengthens those entrusted to him with such warnings. Just as the former are bitter to us, so the latter are sweet. Just as they are unclean, so these are pure. We rejoice seeing that such vigilance is in your piety that you have already surpassed the examples of your predecessors who always were themselves defenders of the orthodox teaching. Truly the evangelical testimony shall fit well upon you which says, "The good shepherd lays down his life for his own sheep."[3] Just as you are a good shepherd, so he is not even worthy of being denounced as a bad hireling who is accused, not because he abandoned his own sheep, but because he himself was discovered rending them in pieces.

(3) We were about to add some details also, beloved brother, had we not seen that your thoughts are in complete agreement with ours, and we approve you as a most strong defender in the confirmation of the faith. Everything which your holiness has written concerning this matter was delivered to us in order by our son, Posidonius, the deacon. You bared all the snares of the treacherous preaching, and you strengthened the faith so that the heart of those believing in Christ, our God, cannot be drawn to the other side. This is a great triumph for our faith to show forth our doctrines so forcefully, and thus to have defeated the opposing doctrines through the testimony of the divine Scriptures. What shall he accomplish henceforth? Whither shall he turn himself, who, by becoming a lover of impious innovation, since he desired to serve himself in his own ideas rather than to serve Christ, was willing to injure the people who were entrusted to him by the poison of his own preaching? It is necessary both to understand clearly and to remember that one must flee rather than seek foolish questions which do not promote the health of souls but proceed to their destruction.[4]

(4) Nevertheless we ought to recall, if we can, one who is hurrying toward the very crags, or rather already lingering on the crag itself whence he will fall, lest we shall hasten his fall by

3. Cf. Jn 10.11.
4. Cf. Ti 3.9.

not rescuing him. Christ, our God, about whose birth questions
are being raised, taught us[5] to take pains for one sheep, desiring to recall it even on his own shoulders, lest it be exposed to
the wolf for prey. And so then, how does he, who taught us to
move so quickly for the safety of one sheep, desire us to take
pains for the shepherd of the sheep himself, who, having
forgotten the name itself and the mandate of shepherd,
turned himself into the rapacity of a wolf desiring to destroy
the flock which he himself ought to keep safe? We ought to
remove this shepherd from the fold of the lambs if we do not
correct him, as we desire. It is our wish that there still be hope
of pardon for the one being corrected, so that he may return
and live, if he would not destroy the life of those entrusted to
him.

(5) But let there be an open judgment against him if he
continues, for such a wound must be cut out, by which not one
limb is injured, but the whole body of the church is wounded.
For what is he, who differs from our faith and seems to agree
only with himself, doing in the midst of those who agree with
each other? Wherefore let them share in our communion
whom he put away from communion because they speak
against him, and let him know that he cannot share our communion if he persists in this path of perversion by opposing the
apostolic teaching.

(6) Accordingly, since the authentic teaching of our see is in
harmony with you, using our apostolic authority you will carry
out this decree with accurate firmness. Within ten days, count-
ing from the day of this warning, he should either condemn his
evil teachings by a written confession, and strongly affirm that
he himself holds that belief concerning the birth of Christ, our
God, which the Church of Rome, and the church of your
holiness, and universal devotion upholds, or, if he should not
do this, your holiness, because of care for that church, should
immediately understand that he must be removed from our
body in every way who did not desire to receive the healing of
those treating him, and, as an evil pestilence, was driven

5. Cf. Lk 15.5.

toward his own destruction and that of all those entrusted to him.

(7) And we wrote these same instructions to our holy brothers and fellow bishops, John, Rufus, Juvenal, and Flavian,[6] in order that our judgment concerning him, or rather the divine judgment of Christ, may be manifest.

6. John was Bishop of Antioch, Rufus of Thessalonica, Juvenal of Jerusalem, and Flavian of Philippi.

LETTER 13

To my beloved brother and fellow bishop John, Cyril sends greetings in the Lord.[1]

OUR REVERENCE,[2] DOUBTLESS, completely and through many persons knows of the present condition of the holy Church of Constantinople, that it is exceedingly upset, and many even of the very zealous and moderate people have remained excommunicated, enduring no ordinary disturbance about the faith itself from the things said in that church by the most devout bishop, Nestorius. I also counseled him by letters to abstain from questions so wicked and perverted, and to follow the faith of the Fathers.

(2) But he thought I wrote these things from ill-will. He was so far from heeding one who had written to his piety out of love that he thought that he could carry away an audience even in Rome with such thoughts and words. He wrote some strange things when he composed a long letter to my lord, the most God-revering Bishop of the Church of Rome, Celestine. He actually included in his letter a statement against his opponents that they do not shrink from calling the Holy Virgin Mother of God. Then he also sent pamphlets of his teachings, and, after they read them and after many assemblies had been held, the God-revering bishops in the great city of Rome cried out against him, openly saying that he was instituting a very dangerous heresy such as no previous heretic had invented.

(3) Because it was necessary for me to tell all that happened,

---

1. For the critical text of this letter see Schwartz, *ACO* 1.1.1 pp. 92–93. Geerard numbers this letter 5313 in *CPG*. See also Festugière, *Éphèse*, 137–138.

2. John, Bishop of Antioch.

since his piety[3] wrote to Rome, and to send to him[4] copies of my writings, the beloved deacon, Posidonius, a cleric of Alexandria, had to go abroad. When his statements were read in the assembly, and especially his letters in which there is no room for quibbling, for they have his signature, the holy Roman synod decreed openly and actually put in writing what those holding fast to communion with the whole West must observe. They have also written similar letters to Rufus, the God-loving Bishop of Thessalonica, and to the rest of the God-revering bishops of Macedonia, who always concur with his decisions. They have written the same to Juvenal, the most God-revering Bishop of Jerusalem.

(4) Accordingly it is the duty of your reverence to consider what is advantageous.[5] For we shall follow the judgments from him[6] fearing to slip away from the communion of so many bishops. They have been constrained not by paltry reasons, nor have they rendered judgment and pronounced sentence for slight causes, but for the faith itself, and for the churches everywhere disturbed, and for the edification of the people.

(5) Salute the brotherhood with you; the brethren with me salute you in the Lord.

3. Nestorius.
4. Pope Celestine I.
5. John had tried to make Nestorius change his ways previously.
6. Pope Celestine I.

LETTER 14

To my beloved lord, brother and fellow bishop Acacius, Cyril sends greetings in the Lord.[1]

HOSE WHO ARE MUCH grieved and have a heart wounded by anxieties have great comfort when they tell some like-minded persons the reasons for their grief. And I am such a one. Indeed because of this I thought it necessary to write to your perfection[2] the causes for which, justly, as I think, I have been grieved or rather I am grieved even still. It was not enough for the most pious bishop, Nestorius, to say in church things which gave scandal to the church and enfeebled the faith in Christ, the Savior of us all, but he actually also allowed a certain bishop, Dorotheus, to dare to say openly in church and before the congregation, "If anyone says that Mary is the Mother of God, let him be anathema."

(2) What shall we do in the orthodox church since we have been anathematized with the holy Fathers? For I find the renowned bishop, Athanasius, very often in his writings naming her the Mother of God, and our blessed father, Theophilus, and many other holy bishops also in their days did so, Basil,

---

1. For the critical text of this letter see Schwartz, *ACO* 1.1.1 pp. 98–99. Geerard numbers this letter 5314 in *CPG*. See also Festugière, *Éphèse*, 146–167.

2. Acacius, Bishop of Beroea in northern Thrace, was already an old man at the time. He was famed for sanctity, but two episodes of his life are difficult to explain. He worked against St. John Chrysostom at the Synod of the Oak in 403 (see Letter 2, note 2), and when his plea for leniency toward Nestorius failed he worked against Cyril during the Council of Ephesus. His letters make strange reading as a result. He died at the unusual age of 110 years, about 433. See Quasten 3.482, and "Acacius I" in *Die Religion in Geschichte und Gegenwart* 1 (Tübingen, 1957), col. 82.

and Gregory, and blessed Atticus himself.[3] None of the orthodox bishops, I think, feared to call her the Mother of God, if, as
is the fact, it is true that the Emmanuel is God. The holy
Fathers who are with God and all who, while following the
right teachings of the truth, confess that Christ is God, have
become anathema.

(3) But the damage as a result of the affair does not stop
here, for the minds of the people have also been perverted. I
have lamented as I heard that some have already fallen to this
point of unbelief and ignorance that they do not admit that
Christ is God and that others, even if they choose to admit that
he is God at all, have no true faith in him, but say that he bears
this name by good pleasure and grace as we do. These are
causes for lamentation and wailing.

(4) What real advantage is there to discuss publicly matters
so subtle and hidden? Why do we not rather aid the people by
discourses on moral topics, if we do not have a high degree of
dogmatic exactitude? Since we explained the true teaching of
the faith to the monks in Egypt and Alexandria, who had been
disturbed by such readings, that is to say statements, he has
proven himself the enemy and has become hostile. He gathers
together certain imposters and condemned men and prepares
certain lies against me before many persons.

(5) And perhaps justly. For if we had zeal for God, and if we
were imitators of the love for God which the Fathers had, we
would long ago have taken a stand by issuing a synodal decree
against those who dare to babble nonsense against Christ and
anathematize us the living, and the holy Fathers already with
God. By such a decree probably those whose faith had been
impaired would be healed.

(6) Salute the brotherhood with you. The brethren with me
salute you in the Lord.

3. Atticus, Patriarch of Constantinople, and Theophilus, uncle and prede-
cessor of Cyril, both were involved in the Synod of the Oak.

LETTER 15

To my lord, Cyril, the most holy and most God-loving bishop, Acacius sends greetings in the Lord.[1]

READ THE UNHAPPY letter of your reverence, which was recently delivered to me, one filled with tears and lamentations on account of the common talk in Constantinople. In it the profundity of your faith in Christ prevails and also states, as is necessary, how extraordinary it was to have brought this matter into our midst even in the beginning. What did it profit Apollinaris of Laodicea to be one of those fighting in the forefront, a great combatant fighting powerfully in behalf of the true faith against its enemies? By presuming his own wisdom and by desiring to introduce certain paths out of trackless places to the pure and genuine faith of Christ, did he not bring it about that he was considered among schismatics by the Universal Church? Has it not been said by one of the bishops before us[2] of vigorous mind and full knowledge, because he desired to check well-disposed persons from meddling in matters above man, when he made the statement, "Let the way be honored by silence in which the Father begot the only begotten"? And as his homily progressed he recounted how this inquiry almost escapes all the powers in heaven alike, to say nothing of men and human comprehension.

(2) Surely the advice of the divine Scriptures is necessary

---

1. For the critical text of this letter see Schwartz, *ACO* 1.1.1 pp. 99–100. Geerard numbers this letter 5315 in *CPG*. See also Festugière, *Éphèse*, 148–150. On Acacius cf. Letter 14, note 2.

2. St. Basil in his homily *In sanctam Christi generationem*. See: *Basilii Caesareae Cappadociae Archiepiscopi Opera Omnia Quae Extant*, ed. J. Garnier (Paris, 1839), 2:848, opening sentence and final sentence of section 1, 849. See also Quasten 3.219, 228–231.

and fitting when they explain, "Seek not the things that are too high for you, and search not into things above your ability; but the things that have been commanded you, think on them. For there is no need for you of things hidden."[3] But those seeking to speak on behalf of men who endeavored to think and declare these things say that they have experienced something nearly like that which the blessed Paulinus, the bishop, endured.[4] He refused to say openly three substances (*hupostaseis*),[5] although he implicitly and truly thought so and conformed in these matters. He followed the western God-loving bishops because of the Latin expression,[6] and its inability to express three *hupostaseis*, compared to our Greek idiom.

(3) However, all of us, who can share the distress of the Church of God, must consider it important to repress the formula reported, so as not to give a pretext to those prepared to tear apart and divide the Church of God. Therefore your clear and balanced judgment must calm the disturbance, if it was such to begin with, capable of troubling and disturbing many pious and Christ-loving persons. As I said beforehand, many of those coming from Constantinople to us in Antioch, some clerics and some laity, seem to agree with the reported statement as not having a meaning opposed to the apostolic faith, and to the faith of the holy Fathers who assembled in Nicaea concerning the controversy over the word consubstantial, a faith coming from God and transmitted to the entire Universal Church. Since the crisis calls for it, deem it right to show forth the wisdom, sympathy, and perfection of your episcopal office. If your holiness will act as arbiter for the

3. Cf. Sir 3.21, 22.
4. Paulinus was Bishop of Antioch during the Arian heresy. He opposed Meletius and was confirmed as Bishop of Antioch. His part in the trouble is discussed in St. Jerome's Letters 57 and 58 to Pope Damasus. See I. Hilberg, ed., *Sancti Eusebii Hieronymi Epistulae Pars 1: Epistulae 1–70*, CSEL 54: 503–541.
5. This refers to the Arian denial that the second person of the Trinity, God the Son, is of one essence, nature or substance with the Father. The Arians held that *hupostasis* meant substance, and held that in God there are three substances, of which only one had the plenitude of divinity. The true faith holds that *hupostasis* means person, and that the three divine persons are equal. In his earlier career Acacius had worked against such heresies at Antioch.
6. The Latin word is *persona*, "three divine persons."

meaning of the word with those who have heard it and have been thereby divided, the result will be that you can explain those terms and accomplish what will be possible as the Universal Church is currently tempest-tossed. You can rise to even greater heights if you use the Lord's utterance and rebuke the spiritual sea apparently thrown into confusion by quoting, "Keep silence, be quiet."[7]

(4) I took care that the letter of your reverence be read to the most holy bishop, John of Antioch, and, having heard it with much perception and sympathy, his desires coincide with ours, who are of elderly age, although he recently came to the episcopacy.[8] He thrives by the grace of God on the prizes of contests which are wont to be attached to the episcopacy. All the bishops of the East think highly of him and revere him. He entreats your reverence, as is reported, that your holiness, using proper understanding, treat the adventitious expression as one not to be tolerated. Through the things which you say and through the things which you do, the apostle's words, as the occasion demands, may be proved true, "If I wish to use the authority which God gave to us for edification and not destruction, I shall not be put to shame."[9]

(5) And deign to receive by your innate and characteristic kindness the most beloved bearer of our letter. He is faithful and Christian by ancestry, and in the things of which he may be in need deem him worthy of your customary care. Both I and those with me salute all the brotherhood with you.[10]

7. Mk 4.39.
8. John was Patriarch of Antioch from 429 to 441.
9. Cf. 2 Cor 10.8.
10. Cyril could not heed this wordy and somewhat subtle request for leniency towards Nestorius considering the Pope's explicit orders at the end of Letter 12.

LETTER 16

To my most beloved brother and fellow bishop Juvenal, Cyril sends greetings in the Lord.[1]

 PRAYED THAT THE most pious bishop, Nestorius, would follow closely in the footsteps of men of good repute and would follow the true faith. Which of those who are well-disposed would not pray that the most esteemed may be the ones who have been assigned to guide the flocks of the Savior? Beyond our expectations the nature of the affair has gone past all bounds. The one whom we thought would be a true shepherd, we have found to be a persecutor of the true faith. It is necessary hereafter to remember Christ, the Savior of us all, saying, "I did not come to cast peace upon the earth, but a sword. For I came to set a man at variance with his father."[2] Indeed even against our parents this war is both without reproach and faultless, or, rather, even full of much praise. When we have perceived that we contend for the glory of Christ, there is every need for us, although weeping because slaying a brother, to gird the zeal for God around ourselves and almost throughout the whole world to say, "If any man be on the Lord's side, let him join with me."[3]

(2) I exhorted him as a brother through a first and a second letter, not to follow his own thoughts but the true and apostolic faith which has been handed down to the churches, because I thought to remove him from the perversity of his writings. But this remedy of the situation gained nothing. The advice has

---

1. For the critical text of this letter see Schwartz, *ACO* 1.1.1 pp. 96–98. Geerard numbers this letter 5316 in *CPG*. See also Festugière, *Éphèse*, 144–145.
2. Cf. Mt 10.34, 35.
3. Ex 32.26.

become unprofitable. So far was he from wishing to follow the dogmas of the truth that he dispatched a letter to me with his own signature in which he even reproved me as one being harassed, and he has conceded that he said the Holy Virgin is not the Mother of God. This is to say distinctly that the Emmanuel, in whom we have hopes of salvation, is not God.

(3) He thought that he would be able to carry clean away the Church of Rome and so he wrote to my lord, the most pious and God-revering brother and fellow bishop Celestine, the Bishop of the Church of Rome, putting in the letter the perversion of his teachings. He sent many commentaries from which he has been proved to have perverted ideas, and he has been sternly judged as a heretic from now on. Since the aforementioned most pious and God-revering Bishop of the Church of Rome, Celestine, has written clearly about him and has sent me the letter, I thought it necessary to send it, and to awaken your reverence to a holy zeal whetted originally through writing, so that with unanimity and an intense zeal we may gird the love for Christ about ourselves. We may thus save the people who are in danger, and may raise up a church so illustrious, by all having become clearly harmonious to all others, and by writing a letter according to a defined form to him and to the people. If, on the one hand, we should save him and set him free from the things which he has thought against the truth, we have gained a brother and have saved a shepherd. But if, on the other hand, our advice should become unprofitable, since he himself has set down in writing the result for himself, he shall eat the fruits of his own labors.

(4) Moreover we ought to write to the Christ-loving and most reverend emperor and to all those in authority. We should advise them not to honor the man above their reverence for Christ, but to conciliate the certainty in the world towards the faith, and for the lambs to get rid of a wicked shepherd, if he does not submit to the counsels of everyone.

(5) Salute the brotherhood with you; that with me salutes you in the Lord.

LETTER 17

Third Letter to Nestorius

To the most pious and most God-loving fellow bishop Nestorius, Cyril and the synod assembled in Alexandria from the diocese of Egypt send greetings in the Lord.[1]

 INCE OUR SAVIOR distinctly says, "He who loves father or mother more than me is not worthy of me; and he who loves son or daughter more than me is not worthy of me,"[2] what shall we suffer who are demanded by your reverence to love you more than Christ, the Savior of us all? Who on the day of judgment will be able to help us? What kind of defense shall we find, if we valued silence so long about the blasphemies which came to be on your part against him? If you injured only yourself by thinking and teaching such things, our concern would be less. You have scandalized the whole church and you have cast a leaven of strange and foreign heresy among the people, not only among those there (i.e., at Constantinople) but everywhere.

(2) The books of your statements were handed round. What kind of an account will suffice for the silence of those with us, or how is it not necessary to remember Christ saying, "Do not think that I have come to send peace upon the earth, but a sword. For I came to set a man at variance with his father, and a daughter with her mother"?[3] When the faith is being injured, let reverence towards parents be dismissed as obsolete and unstable! Let the law of warm affection towards children

---

1. For the critical text of this letter see Schwartz, *ACO* 1.1.1 pp. 33–42. Geerard numbers this letter 5317 in *CPG*. See also Festugière, *Éphèse*, 57–68 and Wickham, *Select Letters*, 12–33.
2. Mt 10.37.
3. Cf. Mt 10.34, 35.

and kinsmen be silenced! Let death hereafter be better for the pious than life, "that they might find a better resurrection"[4] according to the Scriptures!

(3) Therefore, together with the holy synod which has been assembled in the great city of Rome with our most holy and God-revering brother and fellow servant, Celestine the Bishop, presiding, we also solemnly charge you by this third letter, advising you to desist from the doctrines, so wicked and perverted, which you think and teach. Choose instead the true faith, the one handed down to the churches from the beginning through the holy apostles and evangelists, who have been eyewitnesses and servants of the word. If your reverence does not do this, according to the time defined and limited in the letter of the aforementioned most holy and most God-revering brother and fellow minister of ours, Celestine, the Bishop of the Church of Rome, know you that you have no clerical office among us, nor place, nor esteem among the priests of God and the bishops.

(4) It is not possible for us to disregard churches so disturbed, and people scandalized, and true faith being set aside, and flocks being torn asunder by you who ought to preserve them, if you were with us a lover of the true faith and following the piety of the holy Fathers. But we are all in communion with all those, both lay persons and clerics, who were excommunicated for the faith by your reverence or deposed. It is not just, that they who have been known to hold true doctrines be injured by your decrees, because they, in doing the right, have contradicted you. You have made known this very thing in your letter, written by you to our most holy fellow bishop of the great city of Rome, Celestine.

(5) But it shall not suffice for your reverence to confess with us just the profession of the faith set forth in the Holy Spirit during critical times by the holy and great synod assembled in the city of Nicaea. You have not understood and have not interpreted it rightly, but rather perversely, even if you confess the text with your lips. But you must follow up in writing and

4. Heb 11.35.

under oath confess that you also anathematize, on the one hand, your abominable and profane teachings, and, on the other hand, you will teach and think what we, all the bishops throughout the West and the East, teachers and leaders of the laity, [think and teach]. The holy synod in Rome and we all agreed that the letters to your reverence from the Church of Alexandria were orthodox and blameless. But we subjoined to these writings of ours what it is necessary to think and teach, and the teachings from which it is necessary to desist.

(6) For this is the faith of the Catholic and Apostolic Church to which all the orthodox bishops throughout the West and East agree. We believe in one God, the Father almighty, creator of all things both visible and invisible, and in one Lord Jesus Christ, the only begotten Son of God, begotten of the Father, that is of the same substance as the Father, God of God, light of light, true God of true God, begotten not made, consubstantial with the Father, by whom all things were made both those in heaven and those on earth, who for us men and our salvation descended, and was incarnate, and was made man, suffered and rose on the third day, ascended into heaven, and is coming to judge the living and the dead; and in the Holy Spirit.

(7) But those who say: there was a time when he was not, and he was not before he was begotten, and that he was begotten from what was not, or who say that he is of some other *hupostasis* or substance,[5] and say that the Son of God was mutable or subject to change, these the Catholic and Apostolic Church anathematizes.[6] Following in every way the confessions of the holy Fathers, which they made by the Holy Spirit speaking in them, and following the meaning of the thoughts in them, and, as it were, going along a royal road, we say that he, the only begotten Word of God, begotten of the very substance of the Father, true God of true God, light of light, by whom all things were made both those in heaven and those on earth, having descended for our salvation, and having come

5. i.e., another substance than the Father.
6. This is almost verbatim the Creed of the Council of Nicaea.

down to an emptying of himself,[7] was incarnate and was made man, that is, having taken flesh from the Holy Virgin, and having made it his own from the womb, he endured our birth, and came forth as man from a woman, not having lost what he was, but even though he was born in the assumption of flesh and blood, even so he remained what he was, God manifestly in nature and in truth.

(8) We say also that the flesh was neither turned into the nature of the divinity, nor, indeed, that the ineffable nature of the Word of God was altered into the nature of the flesh, for he is immutable and absolutely unchangeable, always being the same, according to the Scriptures. But when he was visible, and still remained an infant in swaddling clothes, and in the bosom of the Virgin who bore him, he filled the whole of creation as God, and was coruler with the one who begot him. For the divine is both without quantity and without magnitude, and does not admit of limitation.

(9) Confessing that the Word was united to flesh substantially, we adore one Son and Lord Jesus Christ. We do not set up a division and distinguish the man and God, nor do we say that they are conjoined to one another by dignity and authority, for this is idle chatter and nothing more. Nor do we speak of the Word of God separately as Christ, and, likewise, the one born of woman separately as another Christ, but we acknowledge only one Christ, the Word of God the Father, with his own flesh. As man he has been the anointed among us, although he gives the Spirit to those worthy of receiving it,[8] and not by measure, as the blessed evangelist, John, says.[9] Neither do we say that the Word of God dwelled, as in an ordinary man, in the one born of the Holy Virgin, in order that Christ might not be thought to be a man bearing God. For even if the Word both "dwelt among us,"[10] and it is said that in Christ "dwells all

7. Cf. Phil 2.7, 8.
8. i.e., Christ as man was anointed with the Holy Spirit, cf. Acts 10.38, but God sent the Holy Spirit to guard the church, cf. Jn 14.16, 17 and Acts 2.1–4.
9. Cf. Jn 3.34.
10. Cf. Jn 1.14.

the fullness of the Godhead bodily,"[11] we do not think that, being made flesh, the Word is said to dwell in him just as in those who are holy, and we do not define the indwelling in him to be the same. But united *kata phusin*,[12] and not changed into flesh, the Word produced an indwelling such as the soul of man might be said to have in its own body.[13]

(10) Therefore Christ is one, both Son and Lord,[14] not by reason of a man having simply a conjoining to God, as God, by a unity of dignity or indeed of authority. For the equality of honor does not unite the natures, and indeed Peter and John were equal in honor to each other, insofar as they were both apostles and holy disciples, except that the two were not one. Neither indeed do we think that the manner of the 'conjoining' is according to a 'juxtaposition', for this is not sufficient for a personal union,[15] nor indeed according to a nonessential participation, as we also, who cleave to the Lord according to the Scripture, are one spirit with him,[16] but rather we reject the term 'conjoining' as not being sufficient to signify the union. Neither do we speak of the Word of God the Father as the God or Lord of the Christ, in order that we may not again openly cut into two the one Christ, the Son and Lord, and may not fall foul of the charge of blasphemy by making him his own God and Lord. The Word of God united, as we already said before,

11. Col 2.9.
12. Here Cyril used the word φύσις, which can present a problem. If translated "nature," it would be heretical, for it would imply one nature in Christ, exactly the doctrine Cyril is at pains to refute. To Cyril φύσις, ὑπόστασις, and πρόσωπον mean the same, a concrete individual, or person, for example his famous formula is, Christ is the one incarnate φύσις of the Word of God, yet later in this letter (cf. note 17, infra) he used the word ὑπόστασις in this formula. When speaking of the humanity of Christ, Cyril usually used the word σάρξ, following Jn 1.14, and when speaking of the incarnate Word, he used the term φύσις σεσαρκομένη. See Letter 40, note 22 and Quasten 3.139.
13. Cyril frequently used the comparison of the union between the soul and body of man to illustrate the intimate union of the Word and Mary's Son, and to show that there is no fusion of the divine and human in Christ.
14. Cf. 1 Cor 8.6.
15. Cyril's term is ἕνωσις φυσική which does not mean a physical union, but a personal union in his terminology, cf. note 12.
16. Cf. 1 Cor. 6.17.

to flesh according to *hupostasis*[17] is God of all and is Lord of all, and neither is he servant of himself nor master of himself.[18] To think and say this is absurd and rather impious as well. He said God is his Father,[19] although he is God by nature and of his Father's substance. But we have not failed to perceive that, while he continued to be God, he also became man under God according to the law proper to the nature of the humanity.[20] But how might he become God or master of himself? Therefore, as man, and as far as concerns what is proper to the limits of the emptying of himself,[21] he says that he himself is under God as we are.[22] Thus he also was "born under the law,"[23] although he proclaims the law and is the lawgiver as God.

(11) But we refuse to say of Christ, "Because of the one who clothed him with flesh, I worship the one clothed; because of the invisible, I adore the invisible."[24] It is abhorrent to say this also, "God, the one assumed, is associated with the one assuming him."[25] Whoever says these things, severs him again into two christs, and in turn sets the humanity and divinity apart also. Whoever says these things admittedly denies the union, according to which one is worshipped together with the other, not as one in another. Indeed God is not associated with another, but one Christ Jesus is meant, the only begotten Son, who is revered along with his flesh by one act of adoration. We confess that he, the Son begotten of God the Father, and only begotten God, though being incapable of suffering according to his own nature, suffered in his own flesh for our sake, according to the Scriptures, and that he made his own the sufferings of his own flesh in his crucified body impassibly, for

17. Here Cyril used ὑπόστασις, where earlier (cf. note 12) he used φύσις, another example of their identical meaning in his mind.

18. Cf. Jn 13.12–16.

19. There are many citations, e.g., Jn 20.17.

20. Christ as man was subject to the natural law.

21. Cf. Phil 2.7, 8.

22. Cf. Jn 8.28–30 and Heb 4.14, 15.

23. Cf. Gal 4.4.

24. A quotation from Nestorius. See Loofs, *Nestoriana*, 262.3, 4, 11, and 12.

25. Another quotation from Nestorius, in which the noteworthy words are the verbs used.

by the grace of God and for the sake of all he tasted death[26] by having surrendered to it his own body although by nature he was life, and was himself the Resurrection.[27] In order that by his ineffable power, after having trampled upon death in his own flesh first, he might become "the first born from the dead"[28] and "the first fruits of those who have fallen asleep"[29] and in order that he might prepare the way for the rise to immortality for the nature of man,[30] by the grace of God, as we said just now, for the sake of all he tasted death, but on the third day he came back to life after despoiling hell. Wherefore, even if the resurrection of the dead may be said to be through a man,[31] still we mean that the man is the Word begotten of God, and that the power of death has been destroyed through him, and he will come at the right time as the one Son and Lord in the glory of the Father to judge the world in justice, as it is written.[32]

(12) But of necessity we shall add this also. Proclaiming the death according to the flesh[33] of the only begotten Son of God, that is, of Jesus Christ, and confessing his Resurrection from the dead and his Ascension into heaven, we celebrate the unbloody sacrifice in the churches, and we thus approach the spiritual blessings and are made holy, becoming partakers of the holy flesh and of the precious blood of Christ, the Savior of us all. And we do this, not as men receiving common flesh, far from it, nor truly the flesh of a man sanctified and conjoined to the Word according to a unity of dignity, or as one having had a divine indwelling, but as the truly life-giving and very own flesh of the Word himself. For, being life according to nature as God, when he was made one with his own flesh, He proclaimed it life-giving. Wherefore even if he may say to us, "Amen, I say to you: Except you eat the flesh of the Son of Man, and drink his blood,"[34] we shall not conclude that his flesh

26. Cf. Heb 2.9.
27. Cf. Acts 4.2.
28. Col 1.18.
29. 1 Cor 15.20.
30. Cf. 1 Cor 15.53.
31. Jn 11.25.
32. Cf. Ps 97(98).9 and cf. Acts 17.31.
33. Cf. 1 Cor 11.26.
34. Cf. Jn 6.53.

is of some one as of a man who is one of us, (for how will the flesh of a man be life-giving according to its own nature?), but as being truly the very flesh of the Son who was both made man and named man for us.

(13) Moreover, we do not allocate the statements of our Savior in the Gospels either to two *hupostaseis* or indeed to two persons, for the one and only Christ is not twofold, even if he be considered as from two entities and they different, which had been made into an inseparable unity, just as, of course, man also is considered to be of soul and body yet is not twofold, but rather one from both. But, because we think rightly, we shall maintain that the statements as man and also the statements as God have been made by one person.

(14) When as God he says about himself, "he who has seen me, has seen the Father,"[35] and, "I and the Father are one,"[36] we think of his divine and ineffable nature according to which he is one with his Father through identity of substance and is his likeness and image and the brightness of his glory.[37] But when, not despising the full measure of his humanity, he said to the Jews, "But now you are seeking to kill me, one who has spoken the truth to you,"[38] again nevertheless even from the full measure of his humanity we recognize the Word who is God in both equality and likeness to his Father. If we must believe that, although he was God by nature, he was made flesh, that is to say, he was made man animated by a rational soul, what reason would anyone have for being ashamed at statements by him, if they had been made by him as man? For if he declined the words which are proper to a man, what necessary reason was there for him becoming man as we are? For what reason would he, who descended for us into a voluntary emptying of himself,[39] decline words proper to the emptying? Therefore to one person must all the statements in the Gospels be ascribed, to the one incarnate *hupostasis* of the Word, for the Lord Jesus Christ is one, according to the Scriptures.[40]

35. Jn 14.9.
36. Jn 10.30.
37. Cf. Heb 1.3.
38. Jn 8.40.
39. Cf. Phil 2.7, 8.
40. Cf. 1 Cor 8.6. See anathema 4 at the end of this letter.

(15) But if he may be called the "apostle and high-priest of our confession"[41] as the one offering to God the Father the confession of the faith being conveyed by us to him and through him to God the Father, and also to the Holy Spirit, again we say that he is by nature the only begotten Son of God. And we do not assign to a man different from him the name and reality of his priesthood, for he became mediator of God and men[42] and conciliator unto peace having offered himself to God the Father for an odor of sweetness.[43] Wherefore he also said, "Sacrifice and oblation you did not want: but a body you have fitted to me. In holocausts and sin-offerings you have had no pleasure. Then said I, 'Behold I come (in the head of the book it is written of me) to do your will, O God.'"[44] For he has offered his own body for an odor of sweetness for our sake rather than his own. What oblation or sacrifice did he need for his own sake, who, since he is God, is superior to all sin? For "if all have sinned and have need of the glory of God"[45] consequently we are apt to fall and the nature of man was weakened toward sin. But he was not so, and we are inferior to his glory because of this. How then would there be a doubt remaining that the true lamb has been sacrificed through us and for our sake? The statement that he has offered himself for his own sake and for ours in no way would escape an accusation for impiety. He has erred in no fashion, nor did he commit sin. Of what sacrifice, therefore, did he have need, since there existed no sin for which, and very reasonably, a sacrifice might exist?

(16) But when he says concerning the Spirit: "He will glorify me,"[46] we, rightly, do not say that the one Christ and Son of God, because he was in need of glory from another, gained glory from the Holy Spirit, since his Spirit is not superior to him nor above him. But since he used the Holy Spirit as a proof of his divinity for the performance of great works, he says that

41. Cf. Heb 3.1.
42. Cf. 1 Tm 2.5.
43. Cf. Eph 5.2.
44. Heb 10.5–7 and cf. Ps 39(40).7–9.
45. Cf. Rom 3.23.
46. Jn 16.14.

he was glorified by him, just as if anyone of us might say, concerning perhaps the strength within him, or the understanding of some subject, "they will glorify me."

(17) For even if the Spirit exists in his own *hupostasis*, and moreover is considered by himself insofar as he is the Spirit and not the Son, yet he is not therefore alien from the Son, for he is called the Spirit of truth and Christ is the truth, and the Spirit proceeds from him,[47] just as undoubtedly he also proceeds from God the Father. Wherefore the Spirit even through the hand of the holy apostles worked miracles after our Lord, Jesus Christ, ascended into heaven, and thereby glorified him. For it is believed that he is God according to nature, and again that he acts through his own Spirit. For this reason he also said, "because he will receive of what is mine and will declare it to you."[48] And we do not in any way say that the Spirit is wise and powerful from a participation, for he is all-perfect and without want of any good. But since he is the Spirit of the power and wisdom of the Father that is of the Son, he is in very truth wisdom and power.

(18) And since the Holy Virgin brought forth as man God united to flesh according to the *hupostasis*, we say that she is the Mother of God, not because the nature of the Word had a beginning of existence from the flesh, for, "In the beginning was the Word, and the Word was with God, and the Word was God,"[49] and he is the creator of the ages, coeternal with the Father, and creator of all things. As we have stated before, having united the human to himself according to *hupostasis* he even endured birth in the flesh from the womb. He did not require because of his own nature as God a birth in time and in the last stages of the world. He was born in order that he might bless the very beginning of our existence, and in order that, because a woman bore him when he was united to the flesh, the curse against the whole race might be stopped. This was sending our bodies from the earth to death, and by him abolishing

47. Cf. Jn 16.13.
48. Jn 16.14.
49. Cf. Jn 1.1.

the saying, "in pain shall you bring forth children,"[50] the words of the prophet might be shown to be true, "strong death has swallowed them up,"[51] and again "God has taken away every tear from every face."[52] Because of this we say that according to the 'economy' he himself both blessed the marriage and attended it when invited in Cana of Galilee along with his holy apostles.

(19) We have been taught to have these thoughts by the holy apostles and evangelists, and by all the divinely inspired Scripture, and by the true confession of the saintly Fathers. It is necessary that your reverence also consent to all these and agree to every one without deceit. What your reverence must anathematize has been subjoined to this letter from us.

1. If anyone does not confess that the Emmanuel is God in truth, and because of this does not confess that the Holy Virgin is the Mother of God, (for she bore according to the flesh the Word of God made flesh), let him be anathema.

2. If anyone does not confess that the Word of God the Father was united to flesh substantially, and that there is one Christ with his own flesh and that he manifestly is God, the same one as is man, let him be anathema.

3. If anyone separates the *hupostaseis* in the one Christ after the union, joining them together only by a conjunction according to dignity, that is, by authority or power, and not rather by a combination which is according to a real union, let him be anathema.

4. If anyone attributes to two persons, that is to two *hupostaseis*, the sayings in the Gospels and apostolic writings, either those made by the saints in reference to Christ or those made by him concerning himself, and ascribes some to a man considered

50. Gn 3.16.
51. This text is a quotation from the LXX. See note 2.
52. Is 25.8.

separately from the Word of God, and ascribes others, as proper to God, only to the Word of God the Father, let him be anathema.

5. If anyone dares to say that Christ is a God-bearing man, and not, rather, that he is God in truth, as the one Son and by nature, in so far as the Word was made flesh and has flesh and blood just as we do, let him be anathema.[53]

6. If anyone says that the Word of God the Father is God or master of the Christ and does not confess rather that he is God, the same one as is man, since the Word was made flesh, according to the Scriptures, let him be anathema.

7. If anyone says that Jesus as man was activated by the Word of God and that the glory of the only begotten was attributed as if the only begotten was separate from him, let him be anathema.

8. If anyone dares to say that the man assumed must be adored with God, the Word, and be glorified with him, and be called God by the same name, as if one existed in the other, (for the word "with," which has always been added, forces this to be the meaning), and does not rather honor the Emmanuel with one adoration only and does not send up to him one hymn of praise only, as the Word was made flesh, let him be anathema.

9. If anyone says that the one Lord Jesus Christ has been glorified by the Spirit, and the Lord was using the power which was through the Spirit as if it belonged to someone else, and says that the Lord received from the Spirit the power to act against unclean spirits, and to complete among men the miracles, and does not rather say that the Spirit is his very own through whom he has performed the miracles, let him be anathema.

53. Cf. Heb 2.14.

10.   The divine Scripture says that Christ is the high priest and apostle of our confession,[54] and has offered himself for us in an odor of fragrance to God the Father.[55] If anyone therefore says that our high priest and apostle is not the very Word of God when he was made flesh and man as we are, but as another man apart from him born of a woman, or if anyone says that he offered himself as the sacrifice for his own sake also, and not rather for us only, (for he who has not known sin would have no need of a sacrifice), let him be anathema.

11.   If anyone does not confess that the flesh of the Lord is life-giving, and is the very own flesh of the Word from God the Father, but says that it is the flesh of some one else other than him joined to him according to dignity, that is as having had only a divine indwelling, or does not rather confess that his flesh is life-giving, as we said, because it was made the very flesh of the Word, who is able to endow all things with life, let him be anathema.

12.   If anyone does not confess that the Word of God suffered in the flesh, and was crucified in the flesh, and tasted death in the flesh, and became the firstborn from the dead,[56] since he is life and life-giving as God, let him be anathema.

54. Cf. Heb 3.1.
55. Cf. Eph 5.2.
56. Cf. Col 1.18.

LETTER 18

To his most beloved and most cherished priests and deacons and people of Constantinople, Cyril, the bishop, and the synod which met in Alexandria of the diocese of Egypt send greetings in the Lord.[1]

INALLY[2] AND WITH difficulty we have arrived at the point at which it were better to start from the beginning, we mean our concern for the salvation of all and for the lack of need to endure disturbance in matters of faith. We speak in defense of ourselves because of the indignities to all of you caused by this. We spent the time just past not without tears and were expecting that the most reverend bishop, Nestorius, would depart from his most discordant teachings because of ecclesiastical counsels and admonitions, and, because of the refutations on the part of all of you, would honor the faith with us which has been handed down to the churches by the holy apostles, evangelists, and all the Sacred Scriptures, sealed by the words of the holy prophets to keep it correct. As a result of what he does not cease saying before you in church, and as a result of his statements in writing, we find that he has erred and to no small degree is acting impiously toward the faith.

1. For the critical text of this letter see Schwartz, *ACO* 1.1.1 pp. 113–114. Geerard numbers this letter 5318 in *CPG*. See also Festugière, *Éphèse*, 170–172.

2. The following introduction precedes the beginning of the letter, "A letter of the same Cyril to the clergy and the people of Constantinople, in which he writes so that they not heed the irreverent teaching of the heretical Nestorius and not be in communion with him, if he remains a wolf instead of a shepherd, but rather they should be manly in the Lord and preserve their unwavering faith. Moreover, he writes that they, who were expelled by Nestorius for speaking against his teaching, are in communion with him [Cyril]." (PG 77.124)

(2) We have already been forced to protest solemnly to him through a synodal letter that, if he does not refrain as quickly as possible from his innovations, and within the fixed time appointed by the most holy and most God-fearing Bishop of the Church of Rome, Celestine, anathematize in writing those things which he said in your presence and has placed in books or at least prepared to be placed in books, and these things are even in our hands, he has no place of communion among the bishops of God, but will be a stranger to all.

(3) Let no one blame the delay. For we were not slumbering while so large a flock, or rather peoples and churches everywhere were being disturbed, but we imitated those who have medical experience who do not immediately suggest for the infections which come into our bodies the necessities of knife and cauterizing, but who soothe them at the beginning with gentle drugs awaiting the moment proper for incisions.

(4) Be manly, therefore, in the Lord, and guarding constantly your faith be zealous to be pleasing to Christ, the one and only true Son of God. Remember also our holy Fathers who rightly and with holiness exercised the function of bishops in our midst and who when they were still going about among you called the Holy Virgin the Mother of God. For she bore Emmanuel, who is truly God. "And the Word was made flesh"[3] and was born according to the flesh so that we might be found to be brothers of him who is above all creation. They did not preach to you two christs but one, the same God, Word and man according to flesh from a woman, not a man joined to God by a mere conjunction and as if by a mere equality of honors. These are the cold, unprofitable and barren teachings of that fellow.

(5) Our Fathers said that the same [Christ] suffered death in his flesh for us, and rose divinely treading upon the power of death, and they said that he will come as the judge of all. Rekindling continually this faith within yourselves, keep spotless and blameless. Do not be in communion with that one mentioned before, nor heed him as pupils, if he remains a wolf

3. Jn 1.14.

instead of a shepherd, and if after this admonition of ours which has been made to him he should choose to hold perverted teachings. To those clerics and laity excommunicated or condemned by him because of their true faith we join ourselves in communion because we do not agree with his unjust decision, but rather praise those who endured that suffering and say to them, "If you are upbraided in the Lord, blessed will you be; because the power of God and the spirit of God has rested upon you."[4]

4. Cf. 1 Pt 4.14.

LETTER 19

To the most reverend and most God-loving fathers of the monasteries which are in Constantinople, Cyril and the holy synod convened in Alexandria send greetings in the Lord.[1]

W E HAVE CLEARLY learned of the zeal of your reverences which you have shown for Christ when he was being blasphemed and this in a church of sound faith, and we strongly approved your affection for Christ and your love for his name. But we continue to weep and to call upon Christ, the Savior of all, that he may now destroy the snare of the devil, take the scandal away from the churches, and halt the blasphemies against his glory. But since he is patient, he lavished a time of repentance upon the most reverend bishop, Nestorius, while all were silent about him hitherto, and awaiting what all had in their prayers that he would depart from his new unhallowed teachings and hold with us those which are true, reasonable, and corresponding with the divinely inspired Scriptures, and accept the faith handed down from the beginning to the churches by the holy apostles and evangelists, who are the genuine ministers of Christ[2] and were enjoined to minister his Gospel to all under heaven.

(2) But since he has remained in the same errors, or perhaps went into worse, as was to be expected, piling blasphemies upon blasphemies, expounding altogether strange and foreign teachings which the holy Catholic Church did not recognize at all, we deemed it just that he be reminded by a third letter, this one sent both by us and by our most holy and

1. For the critical text of this letter see Schwartz, *ACO* 1.1.5 pp. 12–13. Geerard numbers this letter 5319 in *CPG*. See also Festugière, *Éphèse*, 532–533.
2. Cf. 1 Cor 4.1.

God-fearing brother and fellow bishop Celestine, the Bishop of the great city of Rome. If he would choose to repent and, in tears at what he had said, to anathematize in writing his distorted teachings, and to confess clearly and without censure the faith of the Universal Church, he might remain as before by asking for pardon and learning what he must do. But if he does not choose to do this, he would be a stranger and a foreigner to the assembly of bishops and to the dignity of teaching. It is perilous to let loose upon the flocks of the Savior a dreadful wolf in the guise of a shepherd.

(3) Be manly, therefore, as servants of Christ and have a care of your own souls doing everything for the glory of Christ in order that the faith in him may be kept true and blameless everywhere. This will set you free from later dangers and will prepare you to deserve crowns at the divine tribunal, when Christ the Savior of us all will receive everyone of you because of your love for him.

(4) "Greet one another with a holy kiss."[3] All the brethren with me greet you. I pray that you are in good health in the Lord, my beloved and most cherished brethren.

3. Rom 16.16.

LETTER 20

Cyril, to the most beloved and most cherished priests, deacons, and people of Alexandria sends greetings in the Lord.[1]

B Y THE GRACE AND benevolence of Christ, the Savior of us all, we safely crossed the wide sea, great with soft and gentlest winds, so that after finishing the voyage without fear or any danger we arrived at Rhodes, glorifying God and saying with the voice of the Psalmist, "You rule the power of the sea, and you curb the surging of its waves."[2] But since it was necessary that we, being absent in body but present in spirit,[3] embrace you through this letter as children, I thought there was a need to send these words to you, and to set down my position clearly.

(2) For I believe that God will grant the rest especially because he is being asked through the prayers of all of you. Therefore, especially at the present time, show your prayers on our behalf as the fruit of love, for I also do not cease to do this, so that God, the Lord of hosts, who crushes all strifes,[4] by setting in order the opposing forces and alleviating all discord may restore us rejoicing to you rejoicing as children. For he is able to do all things, according to Scripture,[5] and absolutely nothing is impossible to him. Cling to the gentleness which is bred in you and proper to you. This will show you to be especially most worthy, who honor a noble and acceptable life,

1. For the critical text of this letter see Schwartz, *ACO* 1.1.1 p. 116. Geerard numbers this letter 5320 in *CPG*. See also Festugière, *Éphèse*, 176–177.
2. Ps 88(89).10.
3. Cf. Col 2.5.
4. Cf. Jdt 16.2(3).
5. Cf. Lk 1.37.

when your father in the spirit is absent and when he is present.

(3) "Greet one another with a holy kiss."[6] The brethren with me greet you. I pray that you are in good health in the Lord, my beloved and most cherished brethren.

6. Rom 16.16.

LETTER 21

Cyril, to the beloved and most cherished priests, deacons, and people of Alexandria sends greetings in the Lord.[1]

HEN I WAS THIRSTING to address your goodness again, time and place for writing were given me. We are accordingly in the city of Ephesus, continuing in stout health through the prayers of all of you, and think moreover that the time of the synod is near. We trust that Christ, the Savior of all, will cleanse his churches of distorted concepts and will restore most brilliantly the true faith, so that all men everywhere, being clean and blameless, by keeping it sincere may raise pure hands[2] in prayer, saying what was spoken through the voice of blessed David, "May my prayer be directed as incense in your sight, and the lifting of my hands an evening sacrifice."[3]

(2) The wretch, that sleepless beast,[4] goes about plotting against the glory of Christ, but he prevails not at all, since his mischief is fruitless, and his wickedness gains nothing. He plots not against an ordinary person nor just against a man like us according to the opinion of the inventors of new teachings, but against God who can do all things. Accordingly let him hear from everyone who loves Christ, "It is hard for you to kick against the goad."[5] For the wretch chastises himself, and will fall into perdition along with his own children. For those who

---

1. For the critical text of this letter see Schwartz, *ACO* 1.1.1 p. 117. Geerard numbers this letter 5321 in *CPG*. See also Festugière, *Éphèse*, 178–179.
2. 1 Tm 2.8.
3. Ps 140(141).2.
4. Cf. 1 Pt 5.8.
5. Cf. Acts 9.5.

pervert the true dogmas of the holy churches have a share with him; they shall not escape the judgment of God.

(3) Pray accordingly for us, so that God, the Savior of all, may grant that we, rejoicing, may be restored again to you in joy. He can do all things, and nothing at all is impossible to him.[6] "Greet one another with a holy kiss."[7] The brethren with me greet you. I pray that you are in good health in the Lord, my beloved and most cherished brethren.

6. Cf. Lk 1.37.
7. Rom 16.16.

LETTER 22

To my lord, Cyril, the most God-loving and most holy fellow bishop, John sends greetings in the Lord.[1]

N NO SMALL WAY does it vex me that I have been delayed these few days,[2] when your holiness was already present at Ephesus. The longing for your sanctity caused by need pressed upon me the more to complete the journey quickly. I am already at the gates because of the prayers of your holiness, after having endured the great toil of my journey. I have traveled thirty days, for such is the space of time of the journey, not at all giving in to myself, though some of the lords, the most God-loving bishops, were indisposed by the roughness of the way, and many of the beasts of burden broken down because of the strenuous trip. Pray therefore, my lord, that we traverse these remaining five or six stages and hasten without incident and embrace your person holy to us.

(2) Paul and Macarius who are with my lord, the God-loving John, salute your holiness and all the brotherhood with you, and both I and those with me greet you most of all. Farewell. Pray for us, my most God-loving and most holy lord.

1. For the critical text of this letter see Schwartz, *ACO* 1.1.1 p. 119. Geerard numbers this letter 5322 in *CPG*. See also Festugière, *Éphèse*, 184.
2. From the contents this letter from John of Antioch should be dated 431, and the place of writing on the way to Ephesus.

LETTER 23

Cyril, Archbishop of Alexandria, to the bishops Komarius and Potamon, and to the archimandrite of the monasteries, my lord Dalmatius, and to Timothy and Eulogius, beloved and most cherished priests, dedicated in Christ, special greetings.[1]

E WERE EXPECTING the honorable Nestorius to come and repent the evil words which he used after he was consecrated, and ask the pardon of the holy council, even if in this way it would be most dangerous to grant pardon to him; for it is not allowed to grant pardon to a man preaching such things, for he perverted the entire world, and enfeebled the devoted faith of the churches. If one, daring to utter a single reviling word against our most revered and Christian emperors, justly endures the censures of the laws, should not he all the more who is totally impious, who tries to distort our holy mystery, and tries to destroy the economy which the holy and benevolent only begotten Son of God the Father fulfilled for our sake, deigning to become man, so that he might save us all, and free all under heaven from sin and death?

(2) However we marveled at the hardness of heart of the man. He did not repent nor weep at the things which he dared to say against the glory of Christ, the Savior of us all. But even after his arrival at Ephesus he used the same expressions and again showed that he had distorted ideas so that, when the glorious metropolitans and most God-revering bishops brought argument justly against him and hemmed him in by the divinely inspired Scripture and showed that the one begotten of the Holy Virgin according to the flesh is God, using an

1. For the critical text of this letter see Schwartz, *ACO* 1.1.2 pp. 66–68. Geerard numbers this letter 5323 in *CPG*. See also Festugière, *Éphèse*, 258–261.

ungoverned tone of voice he cried out, "I do not say a two or three months old God" and other matters besides these trying to destroy the Incarnation of the only begotten.

(3) The appointed time for the holy council has been given as the holy feast of Pentecost by our most God-loving emperors. For the first letter by which we were called has this summons. We arrived at the city of Ephesus before the appointed day, for it was not proper to disregard the imperial decrees. But when we heard that the most reverend and God-loving Bishop of Antioch, John, was coming, we awaited him for sixteen days, even though the whole council cried out and said that he did not desire to take part in the council, for he feared lest the very honorable Nestorius, who had been originally from the church under him, would suffer deposition from office, and perhaps the matter embarrassed him. And experience showed this to be true later; for he deferred his arrival. For some of the very revered bishops from the East with him, having arrived beforehand, said, "Our lord, the bishop John, commanded us to say to your reverence 'If I am late, do what you are doing.'"

(4) Accordingly the holy council, having assembled on the twenty–eighth day of the month Pauni,[2] according to the Alexandrine calendar, in the great church dedicated to Mary, summoned him by having sent most reverend bishops, so that he would come and take his place and defend himself in regard to the matters which he taught and wrote. But he, at first, made reply saying, "I will look and see." He was summoned by a second letter from the holy council when God-fearing bishops were sent to him again. But he did an extraordinary thing and, taking soldiers from the most magnificent count Candidianus, put them before his house to hinder with clubs anyone from approaching him. But as the most holy bishops who had been sent stayed on saying that they did not come to tell him or to hear anything harsh, but that the holy council was summoning him, he used various pretexts as one who was not willing to

---

2. June 22, 431 in the cathedral at Ephesus dedicated to Mary, the Mother of God, with the title *Theotokos*.

come. For his conscience was rebuking him. Then we used even a third written message and again when the bishops from different provinces had been sent to him, again he used the force of soldiers and did not want to come. Accordingly when the holy council was in session, since it obeyed the laws of the church, after reading his letters and statements and finding them full of blasphemies, after the glorious and most reverend metropolitan bishops had testified, "In the very city of Ephesus when holding discourse with us he clearly stated that Jesus is not God," the council deposed him and brought forth a just and lawful judgment against him.

(5) But since it was necessary that your reverence after learning these things communicate them to those who ought especially to know them lest either he or those zealous in his behalf may carry anyone away, I have of necessity made these matters known. But we have also sent a letter of the most God-revering and God-loving bishop, John, written to him[3] in which John strongly objects that he was bringing in new and impious teachings into the churches and weakening the teaching of the holy Fathers and apostles handed down to the churches. But since he is able to say nothing in defense of his blasphemies, he asserts as a protection, "I appealed for a delay of four days until the Bishop of Antioch would be present and they did not grant it," even though John, the most holy bishop mentioned, gave excuses for not arriving. If he desired to be present, for what reason did he declare through the bishops under his power, "If I am late, do what you are doing"? As I said, he did not desire to be present, knowing that the holy council would by all means condemn Nestorius and vote that he be deposed as a person uttering unholy and blasphemous words against Christ, the Savior of us all.

(6) Since, therefore, as I learned, reports have been brought from the most magnificent count Candidianus, be wary, for I want you to know that the memoranda involved in the deposing of Nestorius have not yet been completed on paper. Therefore, we were not able either to send the report which was due

3. Nestorius.

to be sent to our reverend and victorious emperors, but with the help of God the report along with the memoranda will reach them, if it will be granted to us to send someone able to deliver them. But if the arrival of the memoranda and of the report be delayed, know you that we have not been granted opportunity to send them. Farewell.

LETTER 24

Cyril sends greetings to the priests, deacons, and the people of Alexandria, most beloved and most cherished in the Lord.[1]

VEN THOUGH I OUGHT to make known to your reverence more fully the recent happenings, yet because the bearer of this letter is in a hurry, I write with brevity. Accordingly, I am letting you know that the holy council met in Ephesus on the twenty-eighth day of the month Pauni[2] in the city's great church, dedicated to Mary, the Mother of God. Having spent the entire day, finally we subjected the blasphemous Nestorius, who did not dare to appear in the holy council, to a sentence of deposition and removed him from the episcopacy. We who came together in the meeting were more than two hundred bishops. The entire populace of the city remained from dawn until evening awaiting the judgment of the holy council. As they heard that the wretched man was deposed everyone with one voice began to praise the holy council and to glorify God because the enemy of the faith had fallen. But as we came out of the church, they preceded us with torches as far as the inn, for the evening was near; and there was much joy and lighting of lights in the city, so that even women carrying censers led the way for us. Our Savior showed to those blaspheming his glory that he can do all things.

(2) Therefore, after we complete the papers involved in deposing him, we will be hastening finally to you. With the help of God we all are in good spirits and health by the grace of our Savior. I pray that you are well in the Lord, beloved and most cherished brothers.

1. For the critical text of this letter see Schwartz, *ACO* 1.1.1 pp. 117–118. Geerard numbers this letter 5324 in *CPG*. See also Festugière, *Éphèse*, 180–181.
2. June 22, 431.

LETTER 25

Cyril sends greetings in the Lord to the beloved and most cherished priests, deacons and people of Alexandria.[1]

REAT AND DISTINGUISHED successes are brought to completion not without labors. No doubt it is necessary that for every good thing sweat must be caused first. And no wonder if we see that such occurs in great matters, since common and inferior ones are full of care and come to pass through labors. But even in labor we have learned to say, "Be strong, and be of stout heart and wait for the Lord."[2] For we have taken heart that a glorious result attends zealous actions aimed at virtue and we shall find that our reward from God is the gift of spiritual courage.

(2) Accordingly, God has taken away that most unclear heresy which was attempting to lift itself up against all under heaven, and was "lifting a horn against the Most High and speaking insolence against God."[3] The only begotten Word of God extinguished it as if it were a flame desiring to set fire to the right dogmas of the church, rendering useless the inventor and father of it, and removing him from the office of bishop by the vote of the holy council, so that we say rejoicing, "the Lord has done great things for us: we are joyful."[4] Let there be festivity also for the teachers and leaders of the people that the true faith is strengthened and that in all places the Savior and God of all is glorified, since satan is frustrated and the scandals

---

1. For the critical text of this letter see Schwartz, *ACO* 1.1.1 pp. 118–119. Geerard numbers this letter 5325 in *CPG*. See also Festugière, *Éphèse*, 182–183.
2. Ps 26(27).14.
3. Ps 74(75).6.
4. Ps 125(126).3.

caused by him have been abolished. The dogmas of truth have prevailed over a lie, so that we all in unison with one voice may say, "One Lord, one faith, one baptism."[5]

(3) I write these things even now as if to my children, narrating the marvelous deeds of the Savior, so that you may make your prayers more assiduous, and we may be able with the will of God to be restored in strength rejoicing in your joy. I pray that you are well in the Lord.

5. Eph 4.5.

LETTER 26

Cyril, to the most reverend and most religious fathers of monks and to those practicing the solitary life with you firmly rooted in faith in God, beloved and most dear, greetings in the Lord.[1]

UR LORD, JESUS CHRIST, when he endured the violence of the unholy Jews, being reviled, and slapped, and flogged, and in the end being nailed to the cross because of us and for our sakes, beholding all those ill-treating him and shaking their unholy heads against him, said, "And I looked for one that would grieve together with me, but there was none: and for those who would comfort me, and I found none."[2] Something such as this we see has happened now also.

(2) Yet, so that I do not affront the zeal of the truly faithful, he had many grieving with him at the blasphemies of Nestorius, even if some of those ordained to the episcopacy refused his request by cooperating with the heretic and by drawing themselves up against those fighting for him. But Christ will render useless their ignorance or rather already has done so. His blasphemous mouth has been stopped and his most unclean tongue has been silenced since it no longer utters blasphemies against Christ with doctrinal and episcopal authority. Those who were rather ashamed of his friendship and yet did not take thought of the love due to Christ, have faces covered with shame, for this was their due.

(3) But even if the enemy has been defeated, we are still in the midst of what is left of our worry and we need your prayers

---

1. For the critical text of this letter see Schwartz, *ACO* 1.1.2 pp. 69–70. Geerard numbers this letter 5326 in *CPG*. See also Festugière, *Éphèse*, 262–263.

2. Cf. Ps 68(69).21. For Cyril's attitude toward the Jews cf. Wilken, *Judaism*, 54–68.

to God and it is necessary that you, as you consecrate your own lives to God, lift up pure hands[3] and do this continually for us. Reflect that Josue the son of Naue fought against Amelec with the chosen of Israel and that blessed Moses by holding up his hands sought from God that they be able to conquer their enemies in war and battle.[4] Let your service of God be strong, therefore, in prayer. As true children should, assist your fathers who have cut out the false doctrine of Nestorius like some pestilential disease, in order that we, by having a spotless and blameless faith, suspected from no side, can be very pleasing to Christ who endured all things for us and on account of us.

(4) But please us also by letters. Thus we shall receive the most adequate encouragement in deed. I pray that you are well, my beloved and most cherished brothers.

3. Cf. 1 Tm 2.8.
4. Cf. Ex 17.9–13.

LETTER 27[1]

HE HOLY COUNCIL WAS disturbed very much when it heard that our most magnificent and most esteemed count, John, did not bring back all the news correctly, so much so that those who were there (in Constantinople) were making plans regarding even exile against us, as if the holy council was accepting the uncanonical and unlawful deposition from office issuing from John and the heretics with him.[2]

(2) Then, lo and behold, another report was made by the holy council, explaining both that it was grieved by the imperial letter and that we did not accept the deposition from office of the three individuals;[3] and especially it rendered null and void the things done impiously and illegitimately by them[4] and confirmed those done by us. For the fathers of the council explained also by the first report that they had, in the first place, rendered null and void the things done uncanonically by the others, secondly, they considered us and our fellow bishops

1. For the critical text of this letter see Schwartz, *ACO* 1.1.3 pp. 45–46. Geerard numbers this letter 5327 in *CPG*. See also Festugière, *Éphèse*, 379–380. There is no address given in the text, but from the first sentence it is plain that it was addressed to the clergy at Constantinople. The emperor, Theodosius II, wrote to Ephesus and imposed a sentence of deposition on Nestorius, but he also deposed and arrested Cyril and Memnon, Bishop of Ephesus. They were kept apart under strong guard after the council. For these details and others in the following notes see C. J. Hefele, *A History of the Councils of the Church* (Edinburgh, 1883), 3:44–114; P. Hughes, *The Church in Crisis: A History of the General Councils 325–1870* (New York, 1961), 58–67. Quasten 3.118 has only a brief statement.

2. This refers to John of Antioch and the group of bishops which formed a *Conciliabulum*, or synod of its own, and deposed and excommunicated Cyril, as soon as John arrived at Ephesus. Memnon was also deposed and excommunicated.

3. That is, Nestorius, Cyril, and Memnon. The council did not accept a deposition or the sentence against the last two.

4. That is, John of Antioch and his adherents.

as their associates, and thirdly, that they had not changed from this opinion.[5]

(3) But although the most magnificent gentleman mentioned above had done a thousand things so that John of Antioch and those with him might come into association with the holy council, they[6] do not even to this day permit themselves to listen to such a statement. All resist, saying, that it is impossible that we come to this point, unless what was done by the others uncanonically has been annulled and they prostrate themselves before the council as wrongdoers, and anathematize Nestorius' teachings in writing.

(4) The entire council is in opposition to them on these points. Having failed to gain this objective, the most magnificent gentleman, mentioned before, took thought and asked the council to give into his hands an exposition of faith in writing, in order that he might bring it about that the others also would agree and sign it. Then he might go back saying, "I have united in friendship men who have human causes for distress between them." After considering this the holy council even to the last man arose saying, "We do not insult ourselves. For we have not been summoned as heretics. We came to restore the faith that has been rejected, which we have restored. It is not necessary that the emperor learn the faith now, since he knows it and was baptized in it.

(5) Nor did this, moreover, succeed with the bishops from the East. And you know that, although they composed an exposition of faith, they disagreed with each other and are still in a state of disagreement. For some of them agree to call the Holy Virgin the Mother of God in connection with also calling her the mother of a man,[7] while others completely refuse and say they are ready to have their hands cut off rather than

5. After the seventh session the council did not end. Both sides appealed to the emperor. His reply is mentioned in note 1. The council wrote to the emperor a second time defending Cyril and Memnon and condemning the actions of John and his followers.

6. The bishops of the real council.

7. That is, the human being who is Christ. The Greek word used is ᾿ανθρωποτόκον.

subscribe to such an expression. And they utterly disgrace themselves, because they show themselves to be heretics."

(6) Let all learn of these matters from your reverences, and especially the God-revering and most holy archimandrites, lest the man mentioned above, after he has returned, may tell or relate some other report in place of this to delight the ears of certain people. Let your reverences not be hesitant, or grow weary of the toils on our behalf, knowing that this commends itself both to God and to men. For here through the grace of the Savior some of the most God-fearing bishops, although they have not known us before, are ready to offer their lives for us, and in tears come to us saying that they keep praying that they be exiled and die along with us.

(7) But we are all in great tribulation both because of the soldiers watching us and because we have them sleeping in front of our private bedchambers, especially my own. But the entire rest of the council is utterly weary and sick. And many have died. Finally the remnant are selling their possessions, for they do not have funds.

LETTER 28

Cyril, to Theopemptus, Potamon and Daniel, beloved fellow
bishops in the Lord, greetings.[1]

ANY CALUMNIES HAVE come to exist there against us,
some as if a mob had followed us from the baths of
Alexandria and others as if consecrated virgins or
widows had gone forth with us, since they say that it is reported
by my calumniators that Nestorius underwent deposition according to my intrigue and not according to the purpose of the
holy council. Blessed be our Savior since he has refuted those
who say such things. For after my lord, John, the most magnificent and glorious count of the sacred imperial largesses,
came to the city of Ephesus, he condemned those prating such
things, since he found no truth in them. But he saw that the
holy council of our faith had its own initiative, and that it did
not try to please either me or anyone else, but was moved by a
divine zeal and, since it could not endure the blasphemies of
that man, it condemned him.

(2) But when the letter of the most reverend and Christ-
loving emperors was read by which the depositions of the
three[2] were said to be received, we have been kept under guard
since then nor do we know the outcome. However we give
thanks to Christ because we have been deemed worthy for his
name not only to become prisoners but to endure all other
things. For the matter is not without reward. The council did
not endure to be in communion with John, but resists, saying,

1. For the critical text of this letter see Schwartz, *ACO* 1.1.3 pp. 50–51.
Geerard numbers this letter 5328 in *CPG*. See also Festugière, *Éphèse*, 390–
391. Potamon and Daniel were bishops in Constantinople.
2. The deposing of Nestorius, Cyril, and Memnon, cf. Letter 27, note 1.

"Behold our bodies, behold our churches, behold our cities. You have the power. It is impossible for us to communicate with those of the East unless the representations of their hypocrisy against our fellow bishops be done away with, and they confess the true faith. For they are suspected of speaking and thinking and agreeing with the teachings of Nestorius." Therefore their entire resistance is in these words.

(3) Let all right believers pray for us, for as the blessed David says, "I am ready for scourges."[3]

3. Ps 37.18 (LXX).

LETTER 29

Alypius, the priest of the apostles, to Cyril, the most holy and most God-loving archbishop, greetings in the Lord.[1]

LESSED IS THE MAN whom God will deem worthy to be first to see with the eyes of love your divinely favored and holy head, bearing the martyr's crown of your confession. For you, most holy father, have trodden the way of the holy Fathers with watchful eye, and you have taught those "lame in both knees"[2] to walk upright toward the truth. You have put on the outspokeness of Elias[3] and you alone have assumed the zeal of Phineas.[4] You stopped up the unholy mouth of the venomous dragon,[5] and overturned the gluttonous Bel[6] and rendered useless and strengthless his vain hope of becoming supreme by the means of his wealth and you ruined the contrivance of the golden idol.[6] What mouth giving forth spiritual perfumes will be able to voice the praises of your zeal since you have become the equal of your uncle, the blessed Theophilus, by imitating him, and morever you have wreathed for yourself the martyrdom of the thrice-blessed Athanasius?

(2) Just as he escaped the devices of the lawless heretics as if they were crags in the sea by repelling them with his prayers, so also your holiness has stilled the devices of the lawless man as if they were weak tempests by your conscience's purity of life. In this manner also the blessed Athanasius, after many false denunciations which arose against him from the heretics, proved them stale and useless. He endured living in a foreign land

---

1. For the critical text of this letter see Schwartz, *ACO* 1.1.3 p. 74. Geerard numbers this letter 5329 in *CPG*. See also Festugière, *Éphèse*, 431–432.
2. 1 Kgs (3 Kgs) 18.21.
3. Cf. ibid. 7–45.
4. Cf. Nm 25.7–13.
5. Cf. Dn 14.27.
6. Cf. ibid. 14.21.

because of the order of exile brought against him by those who were then in power. As much as their coarse mouths strove to weave their lying accusations, so much the purer and more illustrious did he show himself by his long-suffering, outshining their successes. While weaving for himself the crown of martyrdom by these contests, he proved the consubstantiality and trod underfoot the evil teaching of Arius and upheld orthodoxy and raised aloft the holy throne of the evangelist, Mark.

(3) And you, by using his words, have followed after that saint. I pray therefore, most holy father, that I be deemed worthy to behold with my very eyes your holy countenance and to embrace your knees, and to enjoy the sight of a martyr binding his crown upon his brow in a season of peace. The beloved deacon, Candidianus, will explain to your holiness the brevity of my letter, that is, how everything is with us, insofar as we have been silent, being confident in your prayer and in the prayer of the holy Fathers.

(4) I greet the entire holy council which has bound on the crown of martyrdom with your holiness. May you be returned to us by God in health and happy, honored in the Lord, fighting for the truth.

LETTER 30

Maximian, the bishop, to the most God-loving and most reverend fellow bishop Cyril, greetings in the Lord.[1]

 HAT YOU HAVE DESIRED, your reverence, has been fulfilled. What you have intended for the sake of piety has been accomplished. What you have yearned for on behalf of piety has come to pass. You have become a spectacle both to angels and to men[2] and to all the bishops of Christ. You not only believed in Christ but you also suffered for his sake. You alone have been judged worthy of the sufferings of Christ,[3] you who have been deemed deserving to bear his marks in your own body.[4] You have confessed him before men, you have been acknowledged by him before his Father in the presence of the holy angels.[5] You have crowned yourself on behalf of religion. You can do all things in Christ who strengthens you.[6] You have humbled satan by your patience; you have laughed at imprisonments; you have trodden upon the wrath of rulers; you have thought hunger as nothing. For you had bread coming down from heaven[7] which gave to men life from above.

(2) Since, therefore, we were not cut off from these happenings, for we learned some things by perceiving them here, and others by hearing of your distress against the principalities of those opposing you, against powers, against the rulers of the darkness of this world, and the spirits of wickedness;[8] and since

---

1. For the critical text of this letter see Schwartz, *ACO* 1.1.3 p. 71. Geerard numbers this letter 5330 in *CPG*. See also Festugière, *Éphèse*, 425–426.

2. Cf. 1 Cor 4.9.
3. Cf. Phil 1.29.
4. Cf. Gal 6.17.
5. Cf. Mt 10.32.
6. Cf. Phil 4.13.
7. Cf. Jn 6.50, 58.
8. Cf. Eph 6.12.

we have been promoted to the archepiscopate of this great city,[9] vouchsafe, your reverence, to support us with your prayers, and to teach us basic principles by your admonitions, and to use all good will toward us so that there may be fulfilled in us that saying of Scripture, "A brother that is helped by his brother is like a strong city."[10] Truly spiritual affection is a strong city not able to be overcome nor besieged by the devil either by undermining or by scaling. For it does not give way to the siege machines of satan because it is guarded by Christ, the Lord, by Christ who conquered the world and has prepared eternal blessings for you, by Christ who said, "He who does not take up his cross and follow me is not worthy of me."[11]

(3) Since, therefore, you have become worthy to be guarded by Christ, the Lord, Christ who conquered the world, and because you have taken up the cross and followed him, be not neglectful of intercession on our behalf before Christ, the Lord, considering our fraternal success as your own prerogatives. Farewell in the Lord, and pray for me, most God-loving and most holy brother.

9. Maximian had been appointed Archbishop of Constantinople after Nestorius had been deposed.

10. Cf. Prv 18.19.

11. Cf. Mt 10.38.

LETTER 31

Cyril, to his most reverend and God-loving fellow bishop, Maximian, greetings in the Lord.[1]

T IS FITTING, I think, even now, since your perfection has been consecrated in the episcopal office which we prayed much that you would receive, to say according to the words of the prophet, "Let heaven rejoice, let the entire earth be glad and cry out with joy."[2] For no longer does that "mouth that spoke great things"[3] exult itself against the glory of our Savior, nor does he who was accustomed to do this lift up his horn on high and speak wickedness against God[4] by denying the Lord who redeemed us. For Jesus Christ, the one and only, true Son of God the Father, redeemed us "not with perishable things, with silver or gold"[5] but rather by having "laid down his life"[6] for us and by having offered himself as an immaculate sacrifice "for an odor of sweetness"[7] to God and Father, and by having given his own blood in exchange for the life of all.[8] He was more worthy than all, and in particular above all creation, since the only begotten Word of God became a perfect man for our sake, not by having endured a change, or an alteration, or the oft-repeated confusion,[9] or a mixture or a change into that which he was not, but rather by having remained what he was even in his humanity which is like to us.

---

1. For the critical text of this letter see Schwartz, *ACO* 1.1.3 p. 72. Geerard numbers this letter 5331 in *CPG*. See also Festugière, *Éphèse*, 427–430.

2. Cf. Ps 95(96).11.   6. Jn 10.15.

3. Dn 7.20.   7. Eph 5.2, Ex 29.18.

4. Ps 74(75).6.   8. Cf. 1 Tim 2.6.

5. 1 Pt 1.18, 19.

9. These were the terms used by Nestorius concerning the two natures in Christ. See Joseph van den Dries, *The Formula of Saint Cyril of Alexandria* (Rome, 1937), 70–73.

For he is believed to be, and truly is, the living and subsistent Word of the Father. But come now, as if with one tongue and with one God-loving mind, let us offer to him the confession of the true faith saying with the blessed Baruch, "This is our God, and there shall be no other accounted in comparison to him. He found out all the way of knowledge and gave it to Jacob his servant, and to Israel his beloved. Afterwards he was seen upon earth and conversed with men."[10] For there was not one Son of God the Father who existed before every age and all time, through whom all things were brought into being, and another one on the other hand, who in the most recent ages of time was born according to the flesh through the Holy Virgin, but rather he himself who "received the seed of Abraham," according to the saying of blessed Paul[11] having partaken of blood and flesh akin to us, "having been made in all things like unto his brothers,"[12] that is, to us, in all things except sin alone.

(2)   And we profess that his body, united to him in truth, was animated by an intelligent soul. For we do not subscribe to the teachings of that crazy Apollinaris. But since we uphold the truth, we anathematize Apollinaris, and Arius, and Eunomius, and with them Nestorius. For we have faith handed down to us from above, "as a safe and sturdy anchor of the soul," according to the Scripture.[13] Accordingly we confess, as I said, the one and only and true Son of God the Father, our Lord, Jesus Christ, knowing that the same one is God the Word from the Father and man from a woman; both above the law as God, and under the law through his humanity,[14] in the dignity of the Lord according to nature, in the form of a servant according to the dispensation (of his Incarnation).[15]

(3)   Both the words of Moses and the foretellings of the prophets provide us with this tradition, and also those very ones who were "eyewitnesses of these things from the beginning and became servants of the Word,"[16] and indeed the holy Fathers who were before us. Because they had the word of life

---

10. Cf. Bar 3.36–38.
11. Heb 2.16.
12. Heb 2.17.
13. Heb 6.19.

14. Cf. Gal 4.4, 5.
15. Cf. Phil 2.7.
16. Lk 1.2.

they became "lights in the world,"[17] and "considering the end of their lives we imitate their faith,"[18] that is, we are zealous to think and say the same things as they did, allowing ourselves in no way to be taken from the beaten path of piety. We remember Holy Scripture crying out, "Make straight the path for your feet, and direct your ways."[19] They who honor the straight paths "run toward the goal to the prize of the heavenly calling in Christ."[20] But those who pay no heed to the apostolic and evangelical tradition and honor the newer, useless and truly ridiculous invention of their own mind, let them hear from all, "Pass not beyond the ancient bounds which your fathers have set."[21] For the way of such is not charming but "their ways are perverse"[22] and bring them to harbor into "the snare of hell"[23] and the trap of death. And Solomon seems to me very wise in bestowing upon an indecent woman the face of every heresy, and then saying about her that it is necessary to repudiate and to flee such a woman, "who is a hunter's snare, and her heart is a net, and in her hands are bonds."[24] The good man before the face of God will be rescued from her and the sinner will be ensnared by her.

(4) But we have been rescued from the snare of this insatiable hunting man. We have been saved through Christ the Savior of us all. Because we believe that he is also God and profess that the Mother of God bore him according to the flesh, we go to him saying, "You will revive us, and we shall not depart from you, and we will proclaim your name"[25] for ever and ever. And of all these thrice-longed-for good things the patron was the divine, mysterious and supernal decree, and the intention of the most religious and Christian emperor, an intention which concurred with commands from on high. For it was fitting that his serenity should not only wrestle and defeat visible enemies but invisible ones as well, and shiver into pieces barbarian battlelines, bring to an end the idle peevish-

---

17. Phil 2.15.
18. Heb 13.7.
19. Prv 4.26.
20. Phil 3.14.
21. Prv 22.28.

22. Prv 2.15.
23. Prv 9.18.
24. Eccl 7.26.
25. Cf. Ps 79(80).19.

ness of the devil and, through your reverence, regulate the safety of those who believe in Christ. For the man who was uttering nonsense in the church and opening his unrestrained mouth for blasphemies against Christ has withdrawn from the holy and divine court and your reverence has grown up in his place and shot up as a plant of peace, according to the Scripture.[26] And this is the brilliant function of a reverend emperor, with a command from on high leading the way, as I said.

(5) Accordingly we rejoice with you since you have the true and blameless faith. For a man, whom you know, has arisen to offer sacrifice and much time was provided for you, and experience in affairs has crowned you. He is a man who has spent much time in good thoughts about you, for his most reverend grey head has thus gone past its youth. For it was necessary, it was necessary to give to the very select flocks of our Savior a wise and experienced master, having a mind filled with pastoral skill, one who knows how to graze his flock in a good meadow and a rich pasture, who has been tested in affairs as a trustworthy and sincere administrator. Those who have been accustomed to live thus Christ also suffers to approach him and deems worthy of every praise, but those who are not such he deposes from the ministry entrusted to their hands.

(6) And that this is true can be seen from Holy Scripture. For God says in one place to the blessed prophet Isaiah, "Go get you in to him that dwells in the priests' quarters, to Sobna the steward, and say to him: Why are you so occupied and what is there that interests you so? Behold the Lord of hosts will throw out and destroy you, mortal man, and will take away your garment and your glorious crown, and will toss you into a large and spacious country and there you shall die, and you shall be removed from your function and station. And it shall come to pass in that day that I shall call my servant Eliacim, the son of Helcia, and I shall clothe him with your robe, and I will give your crown to him, and I will give your function into his

26. Cf. Ez 34.29.

hand, and he shall be a father to the inhabitants of Jerusalem, and to the house of Juda. And I will give the glory of David to him, and he shall rule, and there will be none to speak against him, and I will make him ruler in a trustworthy place, and he shall be a throne of glory to the house of his father, and every man of glory in his father's house will trust him, from the small to the great, and they shall depend upon him in that day. Thus, says the Lord of hosts, the man who was fastened in a trustworthy place shall be removed and he shall fall, and the glory which was upon him will be taken away, because the Lord has spoken it."[27]

(7) Therefore, the God of all truly loves the faithful man and the sincere minister, but he who is not such a man, he turns himself away from as unholy. But he will applaud us for encouraging your holiness, and will gladden you with a rich hand by graces from above, so that by teaching aright the word of truth and following after the faith of the holy Fathers you may persevere in high esteem through the mercy and benevolence of Christ, the Savior of us all, through whom and with whom may there be to God the Father with the Holy Spirit glory and power for ages and ages. Amen.

(8) Salute the brotherhood with you, because the brotherhood with us salutes you in the Lord. Farewell. Remember us, I pray you in the Lord, most reverend and God-loving brother.

27. Is 22.15–25.

LETTER 32

Cyril, to my lords, my most cherished and God-fearing brothers and fellow bishops, Juvenal, Flavian, Arcadius, Projectus, Firmus, Theodoretus, Acacius, and Philip, the priests, greetings in the Lord.[1]

E HAVE BEEN FILLED with assurance again, and through the very experience we have realized that "the truth lives and prevails"[2] according to the saying of the holy man, and nothing at all is arrayed against her. Thus she is the strongest, so that she rises up against every enemy and destroys the strength of those opposing her. For behold, behold she has stilled the lips of those who spoke falsehoods, and the darkness of strange blasphemies has ceased.

(2) The beauty of the dogmas of the truth has shone forth, since the most pious and most God-fearing Maximian has been elected bishop according to the decision and choice of God through your reverences.[3] A long life has honored him, since he is not in indulgences and luxuries but in labors for the sake of virtue and his very great concern for affairs has fitted him, a concern, I say, for the sake of the truth and the dogmas of piety. Accordingly, when congratulating all the churches and the people there, I would rightly say, "Blessed be the Lord because he has visited and wrought redemption for his people."[4] It was not possible that the good shepherd be slumbering, so that he also "lay down his life for his sheep,"[5] but as he always knew how to save, he has driven away the

---

1. For the critical text of this letter see Schwartz, *ACO* 1.1.7 p. 137. A Latin version is in PG 77.155–158 and in Schwartz, *ACO* 1.1.3 p. 180. Geerard numbers this letter 5332 in *CPG*.

2. 1 Ezr 4.38 (LXX).   4. Lk 1.68.
3. October 25, 431.   5. Jn 10.11.

126

wretched beast from his sacred and religious dwelling and lifted up a very wise steward skilled in all virtue, whom we also believe will be eminent in all goodness, and will restore the people under his hand to the pure and chosen way of life.

(3) I pray to the Lord that you are in good health and remember us, my beloved and most cherished brethren.

LETTER 33

To my lord, my most beloved brother and fellow bishop, Acacius, Cyril sends greetings in the Lord.[1]

OUR HOLINESS HAS taken upon itself even now a proper care. For your reverence has the intention according to the goodwill of God, the Savior of us all, that the churches be united[2] and, so that a certain smallness of soul be removed from their midst, that those be persuaded in truth who ought to be of one mind. Everything which saddens them should be removed, and those elements which have been split apart should be bound again in the bonds of charity. But, as it seems, some are afraid of the likelihood of seeming to be clearly in opposition to the purpose of your holiness, but they are either concealing it or they are zealously bringing it about that they are hidden. To do such things and to beg off what cannot be, what else is this than for them to cry out against reality as if the reality of peace is something they do not wish?

(2) And I say these things after reading again the letter sent by your holiness. Through it I learned to seek them out so that every statement and every letter which was completed before the time of the council ought to be rejected by us or approved as being in agreement with the creed of the true faith which was defined in due season by the holy Fathers in the great Nicene Council.

1. For the critical text of this letter see Schwartz, *ACO* 1.1.7 pp. 147–150. A Latin version is in PG 77.157–162. Geerard numbers this letter 5333 in *CPG*.
2. Cyril had returned to Alexandria. Pope Celestine had warned Theodosius to procure peace for the church and he had sent Aristolaus to unite Antioch and Alexandria by insisting on the decrees of Ephesus. John of Antioch held a synod first at Antioch, then at Beroea before Acacius of Beroea, who had demanded of Cyril that, since the Nicene creed was the rule of faith, he should take back his writings against Nestorius. Cyril does not agree.

(3) However, since that creed is sufficient for all knowledge of good, and since there is nothing lacking in it, I certainly will recite it and will agree to it, even if it does not seem to some others to mean or say this. Yet I am completely amazed at this. For against Nestorius who utters those twisted and most abominable statements against Christ, the Savior of us all, and does this before the eyes of the church, we have written what we have written, contradicting him, to be sure, and bringing forth the truth opposite to his polluted innovations of expressions.

(4) And, through the grace of God, after they have read the documents, most men indeed have derived profit and honored in their right mind what was said by us against him. But I do not know why these, who now ought to anathematize his polluted teachings and get themselves apart from his impiety by turning their zeal to everything opposite to him, seek to suppress what was written against him. What reason, I ask, does that have? Let your holiness understand what incongruity the matter contains, if we should reject the things which we wrote in behalf of the true faith, since they are our own, or even more particularly, if we shall find fault with their faith. Therefore, if what was written against Nestorius is not correct, or what was written against his perverse teachings is not correct, then he was deposed from office without cause, even more, also, he perhaps is, indeed, truly wise.

(5) Moreover, then, we erred by not agreeing with him, and more than that by writing against the things which he said. And certainly many books of Nestorius were carried around confusing everything and disturbing the churches. Finally, how shall we destroy those things which were written against him, which perhaps happened to bring help, however brief, to some people? Therefore, your holiness, who is filled with all wisdom, clearly sees that they seek an impossible thing, and that they are so far from a desire to mitigate the discord between us, that they take the matter back to the beginning of his contention which is incapable of being set out in detail. For why did they not, by coming to the great city of Ephesus, bring forth one decree with the council against him who preached such great impious errors? If they had delayed only a short time, what

hindered them from approving what had been legitimately done, after inspecting the records of the council's acts, and from agreeing, as I said, with the correct decree of all, which ought not to be reproached? But, on the contrary, not being mindful of God, nor of the zeal for which they assembled, for the discussion was not about some ordinary cause, but about the faith through which God the Father saved the world in Christ, to us they have shown all bile and unbrotherly hatred, wantonly insulting us in this the holy and ecumenical council by an excommunication,[3] without a trial, and, as if with the wild right hand of savagery, forcing a sword against me and the most reverend bishop Memnon. For we should reckon that we are in accordance with the truth, and anything which pertains to the rectitude of dogmas pierces us.

(6) In some other ways have we been subject to some faults or sins? Ought we not to have been deemed worthy first of a discussion? A conference? A complaint? And while we all, both your holiness with us and the entire council, endured Nestorius while he for a three-year period wore himself out blaspheming, we worked to lead him away from those blasphemies and to change him rather to accept those dogmas which look to rightness and truth. While, however, he persisted and erred much more in speech against the glory of Christ even in the very capital city of Ephesus, at the end the holy council removed him from the exercise of his priesthood as a man sick with an incurable disease.

(7) However, I want your holiness to recall something worthwhile which pertains to the present time. For when in the great city of Constantinople, your holy synod was gathered at the time when John[4] was accused, and later when there were statements composed in writing by men concerning him, when it might come about that a definition against him would be the

3. Cyril and Memnon, Bishop of Ephesus, had been excommunicated by the false synod held by John of Antioch and his followers after he arrived at Ephesus.

4. This was John Chrysostom, Archbishop of Constantinople, who was deposed by the judgment of the Synod of the Oak which met in a suburb of Chalcedon, a city across the Bosporus from Constantinople.

result, and I was one of the bystanders,[5] I know that I heard your holiness speaking in the following words to the synod, "If I knew that, if we granted forgiveness to John, he would be better disposed within himself and would depart from the hardness and harshness which is in him, I would beseech you all in his behalf." Therefore, your holiness made an admirable judgment again in that instance, indeed one which told the truth. What therefore ought the holy council do which uncovered such an impenitent and stubborn man as Nestorius who fought against the true faith? Because he rightly says that it is proper to agree to the one profession of faith, or certainly to the exposition of faith of the three hundred and eighteen,[6] I also, in addition to these words, say that it was the only intention of the holy and ecumenical council which gathered in the capital city of Ephesus that it affirm the profession of faith seeing that all so confess and believe and teach without anything being added and with nothing taken from it. For it is not possible to add anything to it, or possible to take anything away from it. Because of this, the council passed a decree against Nestorius as one who was not persuaded of the profession of faith, but rather as one who removed or obliterated it, and in no way indeed followed it, but had caused some other things foreign to the dogmas of the church to be sown impiously in the ears of the people. There was action, therefore, taken in Ephesus about this individual petition, while the council confirmed the faith expounded by our holy Fathers who gathered at Nicaea in the times of crisis, and I have sent this, so that your holiness might well know. Since it is right and irreprehensible, the very reading of it will clearly explain it.

(8) However, we have added also the testimonies of our holy and blessed Fathers so that those who approach this matter may know how our Fathers, who imbued us with its mysteries, understood the profession of faith. Therefore, since this was done in such a way by all at that time, why should they not

5. Cyril here states that he attended the synod which deposed John Chrysostom. His uncle, Theophilus, was Archbishop of Alexandria. The date was August 403.
6. The 318 bishops at the Council of Nicaea, A.D. 325.

agree to all the more? For if what pleased all is confirmed by all, peace will by every means be obtained, provided that what was agreed upon shall be contradicted by no one. Therefore, even though many things have been done by them, and very difficult too, and every pretext contrary to humanity has been tried, yet considering that enduring this is pleasing to God and to the very pious emperor, a friend of Christ, and besides that, it itself is useful for the church, and holding the accounts of your holiness as worthy of all reverence the result is that we yield to our brothers what they have entrusted to us. Rather we are seeking whatever seems to be right and good for all. It is truly pleasing also to the emperor who is most loving to God. Let them agree to the deposing of Nestorius by anathematizing his blasphemies and polluted teachings, and nothing else is left to be done to remove contention from our midst, for the churches will welcome one another with Christ bestowing on them the reward of peace.

(9) However, let some men not simply spew out the expressions of foreigners against me. They defame me as one who has a taste for the expressions of Apollinaris or Arius or Eunomius, as they have written about me in Ephesus. Through the grace of our Savior I always was orthodox and I was reared also by an orthodox father and I never shared in those expressions which are those of Apollinaris or Arius or Eunomius, far from it, nor those which are of any other heretic. No, rather I anathematize them.

(10) For I do not say that the body of Christ was without a soul, but I confess that it was animated with a rational soul, and I assert that no fusing together took place, nor putting together, nor a refusion as some say, but that the Word of God is unchangeable and immutable according to nature and insusceptible of all suffering according to his own nature. For the divine is impassible and by no means endures the overshadowing of change, but rather is fixed in its own goodness and has unchangeable continuance in essence. I say, moreover, that one Christ and Lord, the only begotten Son of God, suffered for us in his flesh according to the Scriptures, that is, according

to the words of blessed Peter.[7] But the force of the statements was written only against the teachings of Nestorius. For they throw out what he said and wrote in error. Those who anathematize and deny his evil teaching will cease to object to the documents which have been written by us. For they see that the meaning of the statements only goes against his blasphemies. When communion has been restored and peace made among the churches, when it shall be permitted us to write in answer without being suspected, either for those who are there to write to us, or for us again to reply to them, then we also will be satisfied very easily. Some of those things which were written by us are not at all properly understood by some, and these will be clarified. With the help of God we will satisfy them, not then as opponents but as brothers, because all things are going rightly. And of what we have written attacking the teachings of Nestorius, there is none at all which disagrees either with Sacred Scripture or indeed with the definition of faith which was expounded by the holy Fathers, I mean those who were gathered in Nicaea in their own time.

(11) Our intention, therefore, is directed to peace, and to follow what has been decreed by the most pious and most God-loving emperor. We wish that they clearly choose to agree to the deposition of Nestorius from office, and to anathematize his poisoned teachings and be in communion with us and come to concord with us with Christ helping us to this end, Christ, who is our peace according to the Scriptures.[8] But none of them will agree who say that what we have written against the polluted teachings of Nestorius should be thrown out. Most plainly they wish us to be silent about his blasphemies, since they are buying the silence of everyone. Or perhaps they think that we will be persuaded that we may agree with him, if we deny all the things which are our own, which are correct and stainless and stand against his novelties of speech.[9] If, however, some of those who are there, according to what seems best to

7. Cf. 1 Pt 4.1.
8. Cf. Eph 2.14.
9. Cf. 1 Tim 6.20.

them, lead others astray turning their thoughts to what is improper, let them know that they are convicted by all the most God-fearing bishops throughout the world when they do this. For those bishops all agreed and they agree with what was done by us, as being right and expressed properly, since they themselves are precise interpreters of the divine dogmas. May your piety realize in addition, too, that it is fitting that peace from God be arranged among the most loving bishops who are throughout all the empire of the Romans, so that it may become universal and we by healing the schism may not cause many others. For they will not agree at all if something shall have been done which may not seem consistent, and this most of all ought to be considered. Since all in Ephesus persevered and did not agree to communicate with those from the East,[10] for they proposed that this would not occur until they had accepted the deposing of Nestorius and had anathematized his teachings, how, unless this shall have been done, will those actions stand which pertain to communion? Moreover, which of us will not cry out that we shall have damned our souls and denied the true faith, and that we have rejected what was pleasing to all as if it was incorrectly stated?

(12) Is it not completely proper when peace has been made, that we send letters to those who are outstanding above other most holy bishops everywhere, so that they also by having been made concordant may restore communion with them? Finally who may there be who would persuade them, if something shall have been done other than what is pleasing to all, and in which all have persevered, both of the necessity of considering Nestorius deposed and of anathematizing his most outrageous teaching or rather his nonsense against Christ, the Savior of us all? But when we were overcome with sadness unto excess and unendurably grieved because of what was done against me by the Eastern bishops, and far from the clergy of Alexandria and all the most God-fearing bishops of the diocese of Egypt, my most admirable lord, the tribune, Aristolaus, mitigated my grief so that he created a very easy way of making peace and all

10. The followers of John of Antioch.

came to desire this. And I confess that I am a debtor to his excellency, because he is cooperative with me in all things and by his competent plans has taken away what grieved me.

(13) Salute the brotherhood which is with you. The brotherhood which is with us greets you in the Lord.

LETTER 34

To Rabbula, Bishop of Edessa.[1]

THE MOST PIOUS and Christ-loving emperor directed my lord, the most admirable tribune and secretary, Aristolaus, a Christian man and one who is fighting strongly for the true faith, to unite the churches in peace. The emperor also wrote clearly that the Antiochene[2] ought first to subscribe to the condemnation of Nestorius, to anathematize his wicked teachings and then to seek communion with us. My lord, the most religious and excellent old man, Acacius the bishop, wrote to me a certain incongruous proposition as if composed by the bishops of the East, or rather, if one should tell the truth, by those who share the opinions of Nestorius. While it was appropriate that they agree to what was proper and anathematize the wicked teachings of Nestorius, according to the intention of the most pious emperor and of all the orthodox, on the other hand they seek to render void everything which was written by me either in pamphlets or in books. In this way, they say, the churches will be in communion with each other.

(2) But this is plainly to say that we ought to deny the true faith and agree to the blasphemies of Nestorius. If we destroy our writings which are correct and irrefutably assert the truth and fight for the true faith, then we will approve those which are the writings of Nestorius and we will be admirers of his insanity. But we have indeed understood their proposal. For they are saddened because, after Nestorius blasphemed, ser-

1. For the critical text (only the Latin is extant) of this letter see Schwartz, *ACO* 1.1.4 p. 140. Geerard numbers this letter 5334 in *CPG*.
2. John of Antioch.

mons and letters were written by the orthodox against him. But your excellency will know what kind we wrote, while you may be reading the like of theirs. For with this in mind I sent them to your holiness.

LETTER 35

John and all the others who are with me send greetings in the Lord to my most holy and most God-loving brothers and fellow bishops, Sixtus, Cyril and Maximian.[1]

BOTH EAGERNESS AND concern for all those who have obtained consecration and have been entrusted with the divine liturgy of the episcopacy by Christ, the Savior of us all, demand that they be outstanding in the true faith so that they may teach the people in their charge. This is true, and during the year which has passed[2] from the time of the decree of the most reverend and Christ-loving emperors, the holy council of most God-loving bishops has been assembled in the city of Ephesus because of the discussion concerning Nestorius. There, when they were seated with the defenders[3] sent by Celestine[4] of happy memory, the Bishop at that time of the holy Church of Rome, they have overthrown the aforementioned Nestorius by a vote of deposition, as one making use of an unholy teaching, scandalizing many and not walking upright in the faith. But when we hastened thither, because we found that this had happened, we were grieved. For this reason when a difference arose between us and the holy council and between us and the many things done and

1. For the critical text of this letter see Schwartz, *ACO* 1.1.4 p. 33. Geerard numbers this letter 5335 in *CPG*. See also Festugière, *Éphèse*, 508–509.
2. The Council of Ephesus began on June 22, 431. If the year mentioned is understood as the following one, this letter is to be dated in 432.
3. This is the meaning of the Greek word, ἔκδικοι. In the acts of the council those sent by Pope Celestine are called λέγατοι, a word fashioned from the Latin *legati*. John's term, however, is a good one since they were sent to defend the sentence against Nestorius.
4. This is addressed to Pope Sixtus III, who reigned 432 to 440. Pope Celestine died July 27, 432. Sixtus succeeded him on July 31.

said, we returned to our own churches and cities, since we did not agree with the holy council at that time because of the indictment of deposition carried out against Nestorius.[5]

(2) The churches are being torn apart in disagreement and it is fitting that all be most anxious about this situation. In order that they may be united and every disagreement may be removed from our midst, and because the most God-revering and Christ-loving emperor[6] decrees that this be brought about, and for this reason has sent the admirable tribune and secretary, Aristolaus, it has pleased us, for the removal of all strife and for the sake of arbitrating peace for the churches of God, to agree to the vote of the holy council carried out against Nestorius, to hold him as deposed, and to anathematize his infamous teachings, because the churches with us have always kept the true and blameless faith, just as your holiness, and always guard it and hand it on to the people.

(3) We approve also the elevation of the most holy and God-revering Maximian to the bishopric of the holy Church of Constantinople, and we are in communion with all the most God-revering bishops throughout the world who have and protect the faith.

5. No mention is made of the separate synod held at Ephesus by John which excommunicated Cyril, Memnon and the Fathers of the true council.
6. Theodosius. What follows is the submission of John of Antioch and his bishops to the authority of the Pope at Rome and to his doctrinal supremacy.

LETTER 36

A petition delivered to Cyril the archbishop through Paul, the Bishop of Emesa, sent by John, the Bishop of Antioch. To my lord, the bishop Cyril, in all things most sacred and most holy, Paul the bishop sends greetings in the Lord.[1]

UR MOST RELIGIOUS and invincible emperors manifest the zeal and care which they have deigned to have from the beginning concerning their subjects and especially concerning the holy churches of God and the sacred, pure, and true faith which they received from their fathers. They sent a message in writing through the famous tribune and secretary, Aristolaus, to your holiness, to the most sacred and holy bishop, John, and to our most sacred and most holy father Acacius, Bishop of Beroea. They urge us that either by meeting personally or by a meeting of minds we grant a deliverance from differences which have thrust apart the most God-loving bishops who assembled at Ephesus and us ourselves. We should arrange peace dear to God for the holy churches of God and end the disturbances which happen daily to the churches of God, and agree to the deposition of Nestorius and anathematize his perverse teaching.

(2) The aforementioned holy John and the most holy bishop Acacius received this reverend and Christ-loving document and considered that there are many things that require a meeting face to face with you, so that not much time might be wasted in discussion. Hence they sent me to your holiness to examine with you in what way matters concerning peace might

---

1. For the critical text of this letter see Schwartz, *ACO* 1.1.4 pp. 6–7. Geerard numbers this letter 5336 in *CPG*.

safely be arranged and by the best action the necessary and advantageous end may be gained.

(3) When I came and met your holiness I found you mild and peaceful and, as befits archbishops, ready to arrange matters at hand. Your holiness placed in my hands a written statement proclaiming the true and spotless faith which we received from our Fathers. It was above all worthy of your labor and zeal. Since concerning the condemnation of Nestorius your holiness required acceptance of the document given by you from the beginning, I, being present, have offered in your presence this written document through which I confess that we accept the appointment of the most holy and most sacred bishop Maximian, and that we hold Nestorius, who heretofore was the Bishop of the great city of Constantinople, deposed. We anathematize what was said by him as unholy teaching, and we welcome spotless and pure communion with you according to the exposition given by your holiness to us in a few words about the Incarnation of the Word of God. This you also praised and even accepted as your own faith and a copy of it has been inserted into this written document. And by this pure communion we grant deliverance to all those on either side who have been divided from us in confusion. By the love of God we return to the former tranquillity of the churches.

LETTER 37

Cyril, to Theognostus and Charmosynus, priests, and to Leontius, the deacon, greetings in the Lord.[1]

E WRITE TO YOU about all our affairs; then you[2] write as if you comprehend nothing, filling us with perplexities. I know certainly that I informed you by letter that the most venerable and God-revering Acacius of Beroea, after he had been urged by some of the most pious bishops of the East, wrote to me through the lord, the most magnificent Aristolaus, that it was necessary to suppress what was written in my books and letters, and to agree only to the profession of faith set forth in the holy Council at Nicaea. But I wrote a lengthy letter in reply to this, which you undoubtedly received also. The beloved presbyter Eulogius disclosed this. And now after the most pious Paul of Emesa came to Alexandria, all things have been complied with propitiously, peacefully, safely, and as was fitting.

(2) We have not accepted back those deposed by the God-revering bishop Maximian, nor hold them in communion. Neither have we released them from the sentence imposed upon them. We would not at all grant communion to the aforementioned Paul, unless he first brought a document confessing both that the Holy Virgin is the Mother of God and that he anathematized the teachings of Nestorius, and, having received it, would say in church in a loud voice, "We confess that the Holy Virgin is the Mother of God, and we anathematize

---

1. For the critical text of this letter see Schwartz, *ACO* 1.1.7 p. 154. Geerard numbers this letter 5337 in *CPG*.
2. They were at Constantinople and Cyril at Alexandria.

those whosoever do not assert this; and the son is Christ and Lord, not two."

(3) But since he did not come with a document stating that John anathematizes the teachings of Nestorius and, instead, confesses that they hold him deposed because the letters sent from him[3] contained none of the necessary statements, I said that I was not able to grant him communion, until he should do these things. But since I saw that they were rather apathetic toward this, and that the most pious bishop Paul did not think very highly of this, as well as my lord, the most magnificent tribune and secretary Aristolaus, in order that we might not be thought to be declining peace by putting off the matter unto great delays, we wrote the letters of communion. A document was dictated also according to the judgment of the most pious bishop Paul which the Bishop of Antioch ought to sign also, and I sent two clerics along with the most admirable Aristolaus, with the result that, if John should subscribe to the deposition of Nestorius and should anathematize his teachings, they would give him the letters of communion. If not, they should retain them. The most admirable Aristolaus submitted under oath that the document would not be surrendered. He said that, if John did not wish to sign, "I would sail straight to Constantinople and instruct our most reverend emperor that nothing stands in the way with regard to the Church of Alexandria, but the Bishop of the Church of Antioch is the one who does not love peace."

(4) Wherefore do not give way to being despondent. For we have not been so foolish as to anathematize our own writings. We abide by what we have written and what we think. Our beliefs are correct and blameless, and in accord with the Holy Scriptures and the faith set forth by our holy Fathers.

3. John of Antioch.

LETTER 38

To the most holy and most God-loving bishop, Cyril, John [of Antioch] sends greetings in the Lord.[1]

OT LONG AGO AS a result of the decree of our most pious emperors a council of the most God-loving bishops was summoned to convene at the city of Ephesus on account of ecclesiastical matters and the true faith. But we found what the situation was at our arrival in the city already mentioned and returned without a meeting with each other. It is superfluous now in a time of peace to mention the causes of disagreement.[2] The churches were being torn apart in disagreement in this fashion. It was necessary that all take thought particularly about this, since they might be joined together with all disagreement removed from their midst. The most pious and Christ-loving emperors decreed that this very thing come to be, namely, the uniting of the churches of Christ. For this very reason they have sent my lord, the most admirable and remarkable tribune and secretary, Aristolaus, bearing their pious letter bidding us thereupon to meet directly and take away the scandals from our midst and put to rest all disturbance and all distress.

(2) Yielding to this pious letter, immediately and straightaway we sent my lord, in all things the most God-loving bishop, Paul. Thus I also pleased the most holy and most God-loving bishop, our father, Acacius, and the most God-loving bishops with us. We have done this for the sake of more conciseness,

1. For the critical text of this letter see Schwartz, *ACO* 1.1.4 pp. 7–9. Geerard numbers this letter 5338 in *CPG*. See also Festugière, *Éphèse*, 474–476.
2. This glosses over the rival council John held at Ephesus and the condemnation against Cyril and Memnon.

because we are not able to meet face to face to bring to completion what was decreed by our most pious emperors. We have commanded him that both in our stead and for our sake and in our name, he should give form to what concerns peace, which is the leading matter, and to put in the hands of your reverence the statement, which is in harmony with us, concerning the Incarnation of our Lord, Jesus Christ, which statement we sent to your reverence through the aforesaid most God-loving man. It is as follows:

Adding nothing whatsoever to the faith of the holy Fathers set forth at Nicaea we shall speak in a few words, which are necessarily not an addition but in the fullness of conviction, as we have received the faith both from the beginning from the divine Scriptures and from the tradition of the holy Fathers, as to how we think and speak concerning the Virgin Mary, the Mother of God and concerning the manner of the Incarnation of the only begotten Son of God. As we have said before, the faith set forth at Nicaea is sufficient for all knowledge of piety, and for public proclamation against all heretical evil teaching. We will speak without making a bold bid for things unattainable, yet in the admission of our own weakness excluding those wishing to intrude into matters in which we examine what is above man.

Therefore we confess that our Lord Jesus Christ, the only begotten Son of God, is perfect God and perfect man, of a rational soul and body, begotten before ages from the Father according to his divinity and that in recent ages he himself for us and for our salvation was born from the Virgin Mary according to his humanity, consubstantial to the Father himself according to divinity and consubstantial to us according to his humanity, for a union was made of his two natures.[3] Accordingly we confess one Christ, one Son, one Lord. With this understanding of a union without fusion we confess that the Holy Virgin is the Mother of God, because God the Word was made flesh and was made man, and from his very conception he united to himself a temple taken from her. And we know that theologians regard some

3. For a comparison of Antioch and Alexandria on this point cf. Wilken, *Judaism*, 184.

of the evangelical and apostolic sayings regarding the Lord as common, that is, as pertaining to one person, and that theologians divide others of the sayings as pertaining to two natures, and refer those proper to God to the divinity of Christ, but the lowly ones to his humanity.[4]

(3) Since this confession of faith has been accepted, it has pleased us, for the removal of all contention, and to direct the universal peace in the churches of God, and to remove the scandals which have grown up, to hold Nestorius, who formerly was the Bishop of Constantinople, as deposed. We anathematize his worthless and "profane novelties"[5] because the holy churches of God with us have kept the right and healing faith and guard it and hand it on to the people, just as your holiness does also. We join as well in approving the appointment of the most holy and God-loving Maximian as Bishop of the holy Church of God at Constantinople, and we are in communion with all the God-revering bishops throughout the world who hold and preach the true and blameless faith.

(4) Farewell, and may you continue praying for us, my most God-loving and most holy lord, and most noble brother of all to me.[6]

4. See Quasten 3.138–140.
5. 1 Tm 6.20.
6. In the formal language a note of affection is perceptible.

LETTER 39

To my lord, my beloved brother and fellow bishop, John, Cyril sends greetings in the Lord.[1]

ET THE HEAVENS be glad and the earth rejoice."[2] "The intervening wall of the enclosure"[3] has been broken down and grief has ceased, and every manner of disagreement has been removed, since Christ, the Savior of us all, has granted peace to his churches. The most pious and most God-loving emperors have summoned us to this, who have become excellent emulators of their ancestral piety and guard safe and unshaken the true faith in their souls. They have taken special care of the holy churches, so that they may forever have their glory spread abroad and show forth their reign as most noble. To them, Christ, the Lord of hosts, with a rich hand apportions good things and grants them to overpower their adversaries and yields them the victory. For he does not lie when he says, "I live, says the Lord: whosoever shall glorify me, him will I glorify."[4]

(2) Accordingly, since my lord, the most God-beloved[5] fellow bishop and brother, Paul, has arrived at Alexandria, we have been filled with gladness of heart and very justly. Such a man is acting as a mediator, and chooses to be engaged in labors beyond his strength, so that he may conquer the hatred

1. For the critical text of this letter see Schwartz, *ACO* 1.1.4 pp. 15–20. Geerard numbers this letter 5339 in *CPG*. See also Festugière, *Éphèse*, 486–491.
2. Ps 95.11. This expresses Cyril's joy at the reunion with John of Antioch. The date of reconciliation is 433.
3. Eph 2.14.
4. Cf. 1 Sm (1 Kgs) 2.30.
5. In *ACO* 1.1.4 Schwartz reads "most religious" and in *ACO* 2.1.1, he reads "most God-beloved."

of the devil, and unite what was separated by taking away completely the disjointed scandals between us, and crown the churches with us and those with you by harmony and peace. In what manner they are being removed, it is superfluous to say. I assume that it is good to think and to say what is necessary for the season of peace. Hence we were pleased by meeting with the most God-revering man mentioned before, who perhaps in some way suspected that he would even have no small struggles persuading us that we must bring the churches to peace and suppress the laughter of the heterodox and blunt as well the devil's goad of peevishness. But he found us thus holding ourselves ready for this, that he endured no labor at all. For we are mindful of the Savior saying, "My peace I give to you, my peace I leave with you."[6] And we have learned also to say in our prayers, "O Lord, our God, grant us your peace, for you have given us everything,"[7] so that if anyone becomes partaker of the peace furnished by God, he will not be lacking any good thing.

(3) But we have been fully assured, now especially, that the disagreement of our churches happened completely superfluously and not opportunely. My lord, the most reverend bishop, Paul, brought forward a document containing an irreprehensible confession of the faith and verified that this was composed by your holiness and by the most God-loving bishops there. The document is as follows, and is inserted in this letter of mine in the exact words:

Adding nothing whatsoever to the faith of the holy Fathers set forth at Nicaea, we shall speak in a few words, which are necessarily not a statement but in the fullness of conviction, as we have received the faith both from the beginning from the divine Scriptures and from the tradition of the holy Fathers, as to how we think and speak concerning the Virgin Mother of God, and concerning the manner of the Incarnation of the only begotten Son of God. As we have said before, the faith set forth at Nicaea is sufficient for all

6. Cf. Jn 14.27. Cyril has the two phrases in reverse, probably by fault of memory.
7. Is 26.12.

knowledge of piety, and for public proclamation against all heretical evil teaching. We will speak without making a bold bid for things unattainable, yet, in the admission of our own weakness, excluding those wishing to intrude into matters in which we examine what is above man.

Therefore we confess that our Lord Jesus Christ, the only begotten Son of God, is perfect God and perfect man, of a rational soul and body, begotten before ages from the Father according to his divinity, and that, in recent days, he himself for us and for our salvation was born from the Virgin Mary according to his humanity, consubstantial to the Father himself according to divinity and consubstantial to us according to his humanity, for a union was made of his two natures. We confess one Christ, one Son, one Lord. With this understanding of a union without fusion we confess that the Holy Virgin is the Mother of God, because God the Word was made flesh and was made man, and from his very conception he united to himself a temple taken from her. And we know that theologians regard some of the evangelical and apostolic sayings regarding the Lord as common, that is, as pertaining to one person, and that theologians divide others of the sayings as pertaining to two natures, and refer those proper to God to the divinity of Christ, but the lowly ones to his humanity.[8]

(4) Having read these holy words of yours and finding that we thought thus also, for there is "one Lord, one faith, one baptism"[9] we glorified God, the Savior of all, congratulating one another because the churches with us and those with you have the faith corresponding to the divinely inspired Scriptures and the tradition of our holy Fathers. But when I learned that some of those accustomed to find fault and to buzz around justice like wild wasps, were disgorging villainous words against me, as if I was saying that the holy body of Christ had been brought down from heaven and not from the Holy Virgin, I thought it necessary to say to them a few things about this matter. O you foolish men who only know how to accuse

8. Another translation of this paragraph, entitled *Formula of Reunion*, was published as section 5 of this Letter in Wickham, *Select Letters*, 222.

9. Cf. Eph. 4.5.

falsely, how have you been carried past the truth into this opinion, and how have you thought such absurdity? For it was necessary, it was clearly necessary, to think that almost the entire struggle in behalf of the faith has been waged by us because we thoroughly maintained that the Holy Virgin is the Mother of God. If we say that the holy body of Christ, the Savior of us all, was born of heaven and not of her, how would she still be considered the Mother of God? For whom has she borne at all, if it is not true that she has given birth to Emmanuel according to the flesh?

(5) Let those prattling these nonsensical trifles about me be derided. For the blessed prophet Isaiah did not lie saying, "Behold, the virgin will have in her womb and will give birth to a son and they shall call his name Emmanuel, which is interpreted: With us is God"[10] and the holy Gabriel was entirely stating the truth, saying to the Holy Virgin, "Do not be afraid, Mary, for you have found grace with God. And behold you shall conceive in your womb, and shall bring forth a son; and you shall call his name Jesus";[11] "he shall save his people from their sins."[12] But when we say that our Lord Jesus Christ is from heaven and from above, we do not say such things as his holy body was brought down from heaven, but rather follow the divinely inspired Paul, who clearly has cried out, "The first man was of the earth, earthy: the second man is from heaven, heavenly."[13] And we also recall the Savior himself saying, "And no one has ascended into heaven except him who has descended from heaven: the Son of Man."[14]

(6) Although he was born according to the flesh, as I said just now, from the Holy Virgin, and seeing that he is from above and that God the Word came down from heaven and "emptied himself taking the form of a servant,"[15] and has been called the Son of Man after remaining what he was, this is God, immutable and inalterable according to nature, and, considered one with his own flesh, he is said to come down from heaven. But he is named a man from heaven also because the

---

10. Cf. Is 7.14 and Mt 1.23–24.   13. Cf. 1 Cor 15.47.
11. Lk 1.30–31.   14. Jn 3.13.
12. Mt 1.21.   15. Phil 2.7.

one who is perfect in divinity is also the same one who is perfect in humanity and is known in one person. For the Lord Jesus Christ is one, even if the difference of the natures, from which we state the ineffable union has been made is not ignored. Let your holiness deign to control the mouths of those saying that a mixture or confusion or blending of God the Word with the flesh took place, for it is likely that some are babbling these ideas also about me, as if I have thought or said them. But so far am I from thinking any such thing, that I consider that they are mad who imagine that a shadow of change is able to occur with regard to the divine nature of the Word. For he remains what he is always, and he is not changed, but instead never would be changed and will not be capable of alteration. Everyone of us confesses that the Word of God is, moreover, impassible, even though he himself is seen arranging the dispensation of the mystery all-wisely by assigning to himself the sufferings that happened to his own body. And in this way, also, the all-wise Peter speaks, "since Christ has suffered in the flesh"[16] and not in the nature of his ineffable divinity. For in order that he might be believed to be the Savior of all, according to incarnational appropriation, he assumes, as I said, the sufferings of his own flesh, as is foretold through the voice of the prophet about him, "I gave my back to lashes, my cheeks to those who plucked my beard; I did not turn away my face from the disgrace of their spittings."[17]

(7) That we follow the doctrines of the holy Fathers in all ways, and especially of our blessed and all-glorious father, Athanasius, praying earnestly not to depart from him in anything at all, let your holiness be persuaded, and let none of the others be in doubt. I would have added also many cited passages from them to produce belief in my own words from theirs, if I had not feared that somehow through this the length of my letter would become tedious. And in no manner do we permit the defined faith to be shaken by anyone, or the creed of the faith, defined by our holy Fathers who assembled

---

16. Cf. 1 Pt 4.1. See Lampe, *PGL* 938, 7a, s.v., "οἰκείωσις," "appropriation of human flesh by Logos . . . and of its sufferings."
17. Cf. Is 50.6.

at Nicaea in critical times. Nor, indeed, do we allow, either by us or by others, either a word to be changed in it or a single syllable to be omitted, remembering the one who said, "Remove not the ancient landmarks which your fathers set up."[18] For they were not speaking, but the very Spirit of God the Father[19] which proceeds from him and is not someone else's than the Son's by reason of his substance. And in addition to this the words of the holy teacher of the mysteries strengthen our faith. For in the Acts of the Apostles, it is written, "And when they came to Mysia, they tried to get into Bithynia, but the Spirit of Jesus did not permit them."[20] And the divinely inspired Paul writes, "And they who are in the flesh cannot please God, but you are not in the flesh but in the Spirit, if the Spirit of God dwells in you. But if one does not have the Spirit of Christ, he does not belong to him."[21]

(8) But when some of those accustomed "to pervert what is right"[22] turn my words aside into what seems best to them, let your holiness not wonder at this, knowing that those involved in every heresy collect from the divinely inspired Scripture as pretexts of their own deviation whatever was spoken truly through the Holy Spirit, corrupting it by their own evil ideas, and pouring unquenchable fire[23] upon their very own heads. But since we have learned that some have published a corrupt text of the letter of our all-glorious father, Athanasius, to the blessed Epictetus, a letter which is itself orthodox, so that many are done harm from it,[24] thinking that for this reason it would be something useful and necessary for our brothers, we have sent to your holiness copies of it made from the ancient copy which is with us and is genuine.

---

18. Prv 22.28.
19. Cf. Mt 10.20.
20. Acts 16.7.
21. Rom 8.8, 9.
22. Cf. Mi 3.9.
23. Cf. Homer, *Il.* 16.123.
24. The falsification of this letter was done by Nestorius. See Quasten 3.59–60.

LETTER 40

A letter of the same to Acacius, Bishop of Melitene.

To my lord, my beloved brother and fellow bishop, Acacius, Cyril sends greetings in the Lord.[1]

ADDRESSING ONE ANOTHER[2] is a sweet thing for brothers and admirable and deserving of all consideration among those of truly sound thinking, and I say that it is necessary that those of one faith and of one soul unceasingly should hasten to do this, since nothing is in the way nor indeed does anything rebuff the warm desire and eagerness towards it. But there are times when the length of the distances between, or the scarcity of those who might carry a letter, bewitches us even against our will. Yet when time offers the ability to address one another, it is fitting to consider the matter a godsend and to grasp readily the chance to communicate with those thrice-loved. Delighted, therefore, exceedingly at the letter from your excellency and having marveled at your disposition towards me, I thought it proper to make known to you the way in which peace came about for the churches and to indicate how everything happened.

(2) The most pious and Christ-loving emperor having the greatest possible and necessary care for the holy churches did not consider the disagreement between them bearable. After summoning, therefore, the most reverend and most God-

---

1. For the critical text of this letter see Schwartz, *ACO* 1.1.4 pp. 20–31. Geerard numbers this letter 5340 in *CPG*. See also R. Y. Ebied and L. R. Wickham, *A Collection of Unpublished Syriac Letters of Cyril of Alexandria*, CSCO 359: 20–31.

2. Acacius, Bishop of Melitene in Cappadocia, died about 438. See H. Rahner, "Akakios, Bisch. v. Melitene," *Lexikon für Theologie und Kirche*, 2d ed. (Freiburg, 1957–65), 1 (1957): 235.

fearing Bishop of the holy Church of Constantinople, Max-imian[3] and very many other bishops of those who happened to be there, he considered how the disagreement between the churches might be removed from our midst and the sacred ministers of the holy mysteries might be called to peace. But they said that this would never come about in any other way, nor would they, concerning whom the discussion was being held, come to unity of mind towards each other, except by a bond of unity of faith rising before them and, as it were, rescuing them. They said that John, the Bishop of Antioch, a bishop full of reverence for God, must anathematize the teachings of Nestorius and in writing approve his deposition. And as to what refers to personal sorrows, the Bishop of Alexandria will forget for the sake of love and will consider as next to nothing the insulting treatment he received at Ephesus, although it was exceedingly harsh and difficult to endure.

(3) Since, therefore, the most reverend emperor consented and was greatly pleased at these words, my lord, the most admirable tribune and secretary, Aristolaus, was sent to ac-complish this very thing. But when the imperial decree was shown to the bishops in the East and it was explained that it was in accordance with the opinion of the bishops who were pres-ent in the great city of Constantine, intending I do not know what, they met with the most holy and most God-revering Bishop of Beroea, Acacius, and took care to write to me that, in the manner of the agreement or of the peace of the holy churches, it was fitting that this be effected in no other way than it seemed best to them. This was a burdensome and harsh request. For they wished to undo everything written by me in letters, volumes and documents, and only would agree to the faith defined at Nicaea by our holy Fathers. I wrote in answer to this that we all follow the exposition of the faith defined by the holy Fathers in the city of Nicaea, perverting absolutely nothing of the things determined there, for everything in it is

3. Maximian became Bishop of Constantinople after Nestorius was de-posed. See Letter 30, note 9.

correct and untouchable, and, after the definition, it was not safe to meddle still.

(4) As to things we have written correctly against the blasphemies of Nestorius, no argument would persuade us to say that they were not done rightly. Rather it was necessary that they, according to what seemed best to the most pious and Christ-loving emperor, and to the holy council assembled in the city of Ephesus, make a public renunciation of him who fought against the glory of the Savior, anathematize his unholy blasphemies, agree to his deposition and approve the consecration of the most holy and most God-fearing bishop Maximian. Accordingly, when these letters were delivered to them, they sent to Alexandria the most reverend and God-loving bishop Paul, the Bishop of Emesa, with whom I had a great many long talks about the things said and done coarsely and improperly at Ephesus. Putting these out of my mind, since it was fitting rather to follow more necessary pursuits, I asked if he was carrying letters from the most God-fearing bishop, John. He then produced a letter to me which did not contain the things that it should contain, but which had been dictated in a manner in which it should not, for it had the force of provocation not of encouragement. And I did not accept this letter. And although it was fitting that they charm away my sorrow by apologies for the things which preceded and for the things which were done at Ephesus, they even took the opportunity to say that they were provoked against me through their zeal for the holy teachings. But I heard that neither had divine zeal moved them nor were they ranged against me because they were fighting for the teachings of the truth, but because they were yielding to the flatteries of men and because they were snatching for their own sakes at the friendship of those in power at that time.

(5) Nevertheless when the most God-fearing bishop Paul said that he was ready to anathematize the blasphemies of Nestorius and to agree in writing to his deposition, and to do this on behalf of all and in the presence of all the God-fearing bishops of the East, I was opposed saying that a letter concern-

ing this produced by him would be enough by itself alone for the needed achievement of communion with us all. I maintained strongly in every way and by all means that it was proper that the most pious and most God-fearing Bishop of Antioch, John, should set forth a written profession of faith concerning these matters. This has been done, and the barrier and the separation from one another, misleading the churches, has come to an end. But there was no doubt anywhere that the peace of the holy churches was on the point of dispersing the protagonists of the blasphemies of Nestorius.

(6) And to me they seem to have an experience similar to those who suddenly slide off a ship without knowing how to swim. When the wretches are choking, thrashing their hands and feet to and fro, they lay hold of whatever comes along in their love for life. Is it not true to say that they are violently upset since they have fallen away and are isolated from and are outside of the churches which they thought would be a protection for them? Or are they not vexed, and this unbearably, when they see those whom they beguiled turning away from them, and those whom they had intoxicated, so to speak, with "profane novelties."[4] now becoming sober in truth? And yet one might say to them, and very appropriately, what was said by the voice of the prophet, "Be gathered and bound together, uninstructed people, before you become like the flower that passes away."[5] For why in short have they become the eaters of someone else's vomit, not being ashamed while defiling their own hearts with another's filth? "You who are deaf, listen; you who are blind, look and see."[6] "Think of the truth of the Lord, and seek him in simplicity of heart."[7] For what need have you of tangled inventions and distorted reasonings? Why do you, wantonly insulting the path straight forward, make your own ways crooked?[8] "Break up anew your fallow ground and sow not upon thorns."[9] For being distraught, as I said, at the peace of the holy churches they ridicule those who have not endured

---

4. Cf. 1 Tm 6.20.
5. Cf. Zeph 2.1, 2.
6. Is 42.18.

7. Cf. Wis 1.1.
8. Cf. Prv 4.25–27.
9. Jer 4.3.

sharing their wickedness and bitterly denounce the defense of
the holy bishops, I mean those from the East, and then, by
twisting it around to what is pleasing and dear to themselves
and thinking unorthodoxly, they say it is not discordant with
the foolish talking of Nestorius.

(7) And they even joined in censuring us, as if we thought
the opposite to the things which we have already written. But I
learn that they say this also, namely, that recently we have
accepted a doctrinal statement, or a new creed, perhaps, I
suppose, because we lightly esteem the ancient and august one.
"The fool will say foolish things, and his heart will think
nonsense."[10] However, we say this, that no individuals have
demanded an explanation from us, nor have we accepted one
newly coined by others. For the divinely inspired Scripture and
the vigilance of our holy Fathers and the creed formulated by
those who are in every way orthodox are sufficient for us.
When the most holy bishops throughout the East disagreed
with us at Ephesus and have become suspect of being caught in
the snares of the blasphemies of Nestorius, because of this and
rather sensibly, in order that they might set themselves free of
the fault involved in this and because they are eager to satisfy
fully the lovers of the blameless faith because they know how to
have no share in his shameless conduct, they made an apology.
The matter is far removed from all censure and reproach. For
in truth, if even Nestorius himself, at the time when the need of
condemning his own teachings and of choosing the truth instead was pointed out, had made a written confession in these
matters, would anyone say that he devised a new profession of
faith? Why, then, do they uselessly revile the definition of the
profession of faith, by naming the agreement of the God-
fearing bishops of Phoenicia a new explanation? This agreement they have made both advantageously and necessarily by
speaking in their own defense and conciliating those who had
thought that they were following the novel expressions of
Nestorius. For the holy and ecumenical council which assembled in the city of Ephesus knew beforehand of necessity that

10. Cf. Is 32.6.

there was no need of admitting another explanation for the churches of God besides the one that exists which the thrice-blessed Fathers ordained speaking in the Holy Spirit.

(8) Those who once disagreed with the council, I do not know how, after they came under suspicions of not choosing to think correctly and of not following the apostolic and evangelical teachings, would they by their silence be free of dishonor for this, or rather by answering and clarifying the meaning of their opinion? And indeed the divinely inspired disciple has written, "Be ready always with an answer to everyone who asks a reason for the hope that is in you."[11] He who chooses to do this does nothing new and neither is he seen to be fashioning a new explanation, but rather is making clear to those asking him the faith which he has concerning Christ.

(9) But, in addition to these matters, I learned that the enemies of truth, because they have immeasureably gloomy faces at the unanimity of the most God-fearing bishops, are jumbling everything together topsy-turvy, and say that the meaning of the profession made by the bishops agrees with their unholy inventions, a profession which the bishops fashioned in the true faith, innovating, as I said, or adding nothing whatsoever to what was defined long ago, but rather following the faultless teachings of the holy Fathers. But, in order that we may prove them to be speaking falsely, come, let us parade in public the nonsense of Nestorius and the statements of the bishops. For the test would show the truth in this way and in no other.

(10) Accordingly, Nestorius is found to have completely taken away the birth according to the flesh of the only begotten Son of God, for he denies that he was born of a woman, according to the Scriptures. For he speaks thus, "I was taught from the divine Scripture that God came forth from the Virgin, the Mother of Christ, but I was nowhere taught that God was born of her."[12] Again, in another explanation, he says,

11. 1 Pt 3.15.
12. The Greek word is χριστοτόκος. See Loofs, *Nestoriana*, 277.25 and 278.5–7.

"Nowhere does the divine Scripture say that God was born of the Virgin, the Mother of Christ, but instead that Jesus Christ, the Son and Lord, was born."[13] Since he all but clearly shouts it, how would anyone doubt that, by saying these things, he divides the one Son into two sons, and one of them, taken separately, he says is Son and Christ and Lord, the Word begotten of God the Father; but the other, in turn taken separately, he says is Son and Christ and Lord, who was born of the Holy Virgin? But those who call the Holy Virgin Mother of God say that there is one Son and Christ and Lord, perfect in divinity, perfect in humanity, seeing that his flesh was animated by a rational soul. For, that they [the bishops of the East] do not say that there is one Son, the Word of God the Father, and another again who was born of the Holy Virgin, as Nestorius teaches, but rather one and the same Son, would become clear, and quite easily, from the following. They add, signifying who he might be, that he is perfect as God and perfect as man, who was begotten before ages from the Father according to divinity and "in recent days"[14] for us and for our salvation was begotten of Mary, the Holy Virgin, according to his humanity, that the same one is consubstantial with the Father according to his divinity and consubstantial with us according to his humanity.

(11) Therefore, by no means do they divide the one Son and Christ and Lord Jesus in two, but say that he is the same before ages and "in recent days," and clearly that he is from God the Father as God, and from a woman according to the flesh as man. For how might he be thought to be consubstantial with us according to his humanity and yet begotten of the Father according to his divinity, I say, unless the same one is thought to be and said to be God and man as well?

(12) But to Nestorius these things do not seem to be so, but rather his aim has turned to the complete opposite. In truth, he said, when preaching in church, "For this reason also Christ is named God the Word, because he has an uninterrupted con-

13. Ibid., 278.5–7.
14. Cf. Heb 1.2.

joining to the Christ."[15] And again, "Accordingly, let us safe-guard the unconfused conjoining of natures, for let us admit God in man and because of the divine conjoining let us rever-ence the man worshiped together with almighty God."[16]

(13) You see, therefore, how discordant his reasoning is, for he is filled to the brim with irreverence. He says that the Word of God is named Christ separately and has an uninterrupted conjoining with the Christ. Therefore, does he not say most clearly that there are two christs? Does he not confess that he reveres a man, I do not know how, who is adored along with God? These do not appear related to the statements of the bishops of the East, do they? Is not the meaning of his thoughts contradictory? For he clearly says that there are two, but they confess that they worship one Christ and Son and God and Lord, the same one begotten of the Father according to divin-ity and of the Holy Virgin according to humanity. For they say that there was a union of two natures, but clearly they confess one Christ, one Son, and one Lord. For "the Word was made flesh,"[17] according to the Scriptures, and we say that an inef-fable coming together in the Incarnation was truly made of unlike things into an inseparable union.

(14) For we shall not understand, as some of the more ancient heretics, that the Word of God, by having taken his own nature, that is, the divine, prepared a body for himself; but, following in every way the divinely inspired Scriptures, we strongly maintain that He took his flesh from the Holy Virgin. Wherefore, we say that the two natures were united, from which there is the one and only Son and Lord, Jesus Christ, as we accept in our thoughts; but after the union, since the distinction into two is now done away with, we believe that there is one *phusis*[18] of the Son, as one, however, one who became man and was made flesh. But if being God the Word he is said to be incarnate and to be made man, let the suspicion of

15. See Loofs, *Nestoriana*, 275.9–11.
16. Ibid., 249.1–4.
17. Jn 1.14.
18. Cf. Letter 17, note 12, and note 17. Cf. also Cardinal John Henry Newman, *Tracts* (London, 1924), 329–382 on St. Cyril's Formula.

a change be cast somewhere far away, for he has remained what he was, and let the entirely unconfused union be confessed on our part. But perhaps those on the opposite side might say:

Behold, those who fashion the confession of the true faith clearly name two natures, but maintain that the expressions of those inspired by God[19] are divided according to the difference of the two natures. Then, how are these assertions not opposite to yours? For you do not allow the attributing of expressions to two persons, that is, to two *hupostaseis*.

But, my dear friends, I would say, I have written in the propositions:[20]

If anyone attributes to two persons, that is, to two *hupostaseis*, the sayings[21] and ascribes some to a man considered separately from the Word of God, and ascribes others, as proper to God, only to the Word of God the Father, let him be condemned.

(15) But in no way have we removed the distinctions between the sayings, even if we have made a worthless thing of separating them as attributed to the Son considered apart as the Word of God the Father, and to the Son again considered apart as a man from a woman. For confessedly there is one nature of the Word[22] but we know that he has been made flesh and was made man, as I already said. If anyone would thoroughly inquire as to the manner in which he was made flesh

19. The writers of the sacred books of the New Testament.
20. Letter 17, anathema 4.
21. In the Gospels and apostolic writings.
22. This is the closest statement so far in the letters to Cyril's famous formula, which appears in Letter 45 (Schwartz, *ACO* 1.1.6 pp. 153–154). Cf. Letter 44, notes 2 and 5, and Letter 45, note 11. A discussion of the use of the word φύσις in Cyril is found in Hubert Du Manoir, S. J., *Dogme et spiritualité chez saint Cyrille d'Alexandrie* (Paris, 1944), 124–143. See also Quasten 3.140. Whatever objections there may be to the formula itself, we should not anachronize and expect Cyril to know of the definitions of the Council of Chalcedon of 451. Cyril died in 444. If the whole letter is read, in each instance in which the phrase appears, it is clear that Cyril is totally orthodox, since the context in which it is embedded shows what the phrase meant to him, and how it is to be understood. Cf. notes 25 and 30 of this letter. Read also Letter 46 entire.

and was made man, let him ponder on the Word, God of God, "having taken the form of a servant, and being made in the likeness of men,"[23] as it is written. And according to this and only this is the difference of natures, that is, of *hupostaseis*, to be understood, for divinity and humanity are doubtless not the same in natural quality. Otherwise how has the Word, being God, emptied himself having lowered himself in lesser things, that is, to our condition? Accordingly, whenever the manner of the Incarnation is closely considered, the human mind doubtless sees the two ineffably and unconfusedly joined to each other in a union; but the mind in no wise divides them after they have been united, but believes and admits strongly that the one from both is God and Son and Christ and Lord.

(16) But the heresy of Nestorius is completely different from this. For he pretends to confess that the Word, while being God, was incarnate and became man; but, not having known the meaning of the Incarnation, he names two natures but separates them from one another, putting God apart and likewise man in turn, conjoined to God by an external relationship only according to the equality of honor or at least sovereign power. For he says as follows, "God is inseparable from the one who is visible; because of this, I do not separate the honor of the one not separated; I separate the natures; but I unite the adoration."[24]

(17) But the brethren at Antioch, understanding in simple thoughts only those from which Christ is understood to be, have maintained a difference of natures, because, as I said, divinity and humanity are not the same in natural quality, but proclaimed one Son and Christ and Lord as being truly one; they say his person[25] is one, and in no manner do they separate what has been united. Neither do they admit the natural division as the author of the wretched inventions was pleased to think, but they strongly maintain that only the sayings con-

---

23. Cf. Phil 2.6–9.
24. See Loofs, *Nestoriana*, 262.4–6.
25. The terminology of Antioch was clearer, and Cyril accepts it, showing that the meaning is the same as his own thought. Compare this sentence and the one at the end of the last paragraph. Cf. note 30.

cerning the Lord[26] are separated, not that they say that some of them separately are proper to the Son, the Word of God the Father, and others are proper to another son again, the one from a woman, but they say that some are proper to his divinity and others again are proper to his humanity. For the same one is God and man. But they say that there are others which have been made common in a certain way and, as it were, look toward both, I mean both the divinity and the humanity.

(18) What I am saying is the same as this. On the one hand, some of the sayings are very especially proper to his divinity. Others again are proper to his humanity. But others very specially pertain to a certain middle position, because they reveal the Son as God and man, both at the same time and in him. For when he says to Philip, "I am with you so long, and you have not known me, Philip? Do you not believe that I am in the Father and the Father in me? He, who has seen me, has seen the Father."[27] "I and the Father are one."[28] We firmly maintain that this saying is most proper to his divinity. But when he rebukes the Jewish people, saying this, "If you were the children of Abraham, you would be doing the works of Abraham. But as it is, you are seeking to kill me, one who has spoken the truth to you. This Abraham did not do,"[29] we say that such words were spoken as proper to his humanity. Yet we say that those proper to his divinity and those proper to his humanity are the sayings of the one Son. For, being God, he became man, yet having become man he did not put off his being God by the assumption of flesh and blood. But since he is one Christ, both Son and Lord, we say that his person[30] also is one, both we and they say it.[31]

(19) But we strongly maintain that there are other sayings of a middle position, such as when the blessed Paul writes,

26. Cf. notes 19 and 20.
27. Jn 14.9, 10. Cyril has the last two sentences in the reverse order.
28. Jn 10.30.
29. Cf. Jn 8.39, 40.
30. Cyril accepts the word πρόσωπον. To him, this word and φύσις mean the same in the formula. Cf. letter 42, note 2.
31. The bishops with John of Antioch.

"Jesus Christ yesterday and today; the same also forever."[32] And again:

> For even if there are many gods and lords in heaven and on earth, yet for us there is only one God, the Father from whom are all things, and we from him; and one Lord, Jesus Christ, through whom are all things, and we through him.[33]

And again:

> For I could wish to be anathema myself from Christ for the sake of my brethren, who are my kinsmen according to the flesh, who are Israelites, who have the adoption of sons, and the legislation and the covenant and glory; of whom are the fathers and of whom is the Christ according to the flesh, who is over all things, God blessed forever, Amen.[34]

For lo and behold, having mentioned Christ Jesus, he says that he is the same yesterday and today and for eternity, and that through him all things are; and the one, who is from the Jews according to the flesh, he names God over all things, and besides he says that he is blessed forever.

(20) Do not, therefore, divide in these instances the expressions about the Lord, for they have in the same person what is proper to God and what is proper to his humanity; but rather apply them to the one Son, that is, to God the Word made flesh. Accordingly, it is one thing to separate the natures and this after the union, and to say that man is conjoined to God only according to equality of honor, and likewise, it is another thing to know the difference between the expressions. How, therefore, do the things which they [from the East] say concur with the foolish statements of Nestorius? For it is not surprising if to some also the combination of expressions and the utterance of words seem to fall short of fine precision, for such matters are exceedingly hard to express. In this matter, even the divinely inspired Paul asked God for speech to open his mouth.[35]

(21) Therefore, is it not clear to all that they [of the East] do not separate into two the one Lord Jesus Christ, when they say

32. Heb 13.8.　　　　　　　　34. Cf. Rom 9.3–5.
33. Cf. 1 Cor 8.5, 6.　　　　　35. Cf. Eph 6.19.

that it is necessary to apply the sayings proper to God to his divinity, and again the human ones to his humanity? They affirm, as I said, that he is the Word of God the Father, begotten before ages, and was born "in recent days"[36] according to the flesh from the Holy Virgin. They add that he was begotten according to the flesh through the ineffable and unconfused union, and they believe that the Holy Virgin is the Mother of God and clearly confess one Son and Christ and Lord. It is completely incredible that they intend to say that he is one and yet divide the one into two. They have not come to such a state of insanity that they themselves would reinstate the transgressors by imprudently rebuilding what they rightly had torn down. If they agree with the opinions of Nestorius, how do they anathematize them as profane and loathsome?

(22) But I think it is necessary to tell the reasons why those [of the East] came to such a degree of subtlety. For the supporters of the impiety of Arius, wickedly adulterating the meaning of the truth, say that the Word of God became man but that he availed himself of a body without a soul, and they do this out of a love of maliciousness in order that, by assigning to him the human sayings, they might show to those being led astray by them that he is in a lesser position than the excellence of the Father and declare him to be of a different nature from the Father. Because of this the bishops of the East, fearing that the glory and the nature of God the Word might be belittled on account of the things said about him humanly through the Incarnation, separate the sayings, not cutting into two persons, as I said, the one Son and Lord, but applying some sayings to his divinity and again others to his humanity; yet entirely all to one.

(23) But I learned that the most pious and God-fearing bishop, John, wrote to some of his associates as if I clearly taught and in a clear voice confessed the difference of the natures, but divided the sayings in correspondence to the natures, and for this very reason, some were scandalized. It was necessary, therefore, that we speak about this. Your excel-

36. Cf. Heb 1.2.

lency has not been ignorant that those, who pour down on my letters the censure of the opinion of Apollinaris, thought that I say that the holy body of Christ is without a soul, and that a mixture or a confusion or a blending or a change of God the Word was made into flesh, or a passing over of the flesh into the nature of divinity, so that nothing is preserved pure or is what it is. And they thought that, in addition to this, I agreed with the blasphemies of Arius through unwillingness to understand the difference of the sayings and that I say that some are proper to divinity, but others are human and fitted rather to the Incarnation. But that I am free of such errors, your excellency would bear witness to the others.

(24) Yet it was necessary that a defense be made because of those scandalized. For this reason, I wrote to his reverence that I never had the opinions of Arius and Apollinaris and do not indeed say that the Word of God was changed into flesh, but neither do I say that the flesh was transformed into the nature of divinity, because the Word of God is immutable and incomprehensible. The opposite is impossible. But neither did I do away with the difference of the sayings, but I know that the Lord speaks in a manner proper to his divinity, and humanly at the same time, since he is in himself both God and man. Therefore, because he[37] desires to signify this, he wrote that he taught to confess the difference of the natures and to separate the sayings in correspondence to the natures. But such statements are not mine, but have been uttered by him.

(25) And I think to what has been said the following should be added of necessity. For the most God-fearing Bishop of Emesa, Paul, came to me and then, after a discussion had been started concerning the true and blameless faith, questioned me rather earnestly if I approved the letter from our thrice-blessed father of famous memory, Athanasius, to Epictetus, the Bishop of Corinth. I said that, "if the document is preserved with you incorrupt," for many things in it have been falsified by the enemies of the truth,[38] I would approve it by all

37. John of Antioch.
38. By the followers of Nestorius. See Letter 39 at the end, and Letter 45, note 19.

means and in every way. But he said in answer to this that he himself had the letter and that he wished to be fully assured from the copies with us and to learn whether their copies have been corrupted or not. And taking the ancient copies and comparing them with those which he brought, he found that the latter have been corrupted; and he begged that we make copies of the texts with us and send them to the Church of Antioch. And this has been done.

(26) And this is what the most pious and most God-loving bishop, John, wrote about me to Carrenus, namely, that "he expounded the doctrines concerning the Incarnation, and with us wove together the tradition of the Fathers, a tradition which almost was in danger, so to speak, of becoming extinct among men." But if some people carry around a letter, as if it had been written by Philip, the most pious priest of the Church of Rome, to the effect that the most holy bishop Sixtus,[39] was vexed at the deposition of Nestorius and was helping him, let your holiness put no faith in it. For he wrote in agreement with the holy council and maintained everything done by it and is of the same mind as we are.

(27) But if a letter is carried around by some people, as if written by me, to the effect that I changed my mind on the things which we have done at Ephesus, let this also be ridiculed. For we are, through the grace of the Savior, in good health of mind, nor have we come to the end of the proper use of reason.

(28) Salute the brotherhood with you; the brethren with us salute you in the Lord.[40]

39. Pope Sixtus III.
40. For a discussion of Cyril's objections to the heretical terms referred to in this letter cf. H. A. Wolfson, *The Philosophy of the Church Fathers*, 3d rev. ed. (Cambridge, Mass., 1970), 1:407–418.

LETTER 41

A copy of the letter written from him [Cyril] to Acacius, the bishop, concerning the scapegoat.[1]

 WAS PLEASED VERY much to receive the letters sent by your holiness[2] recently, and I almost clasped and kissed them. In the state of mind which I reached you somehow did not seem to be far away. The communications of sincere men are enough to produce such a thought. These are my reactions at the moment and I am persuaded that the thoughts of your holiness are not different. I had to say this since you have deigned to ask that I ought to give some account about the scapegoat.

(2) By this the mystery concerning it may be clarified. Since your wisdom sufficiently possesses the quickness at learning and well-ordered knowledge of the holy Scriptures and esteemed understanding, it is superfluous perhaps to mention anything by someone else concerning the matters being investigated. Since there is no problem in my saying what comes into my mind also, I have written to you, for it was not possible to refuse the assignment. But if it happens that somehow I miss my aim slightly in my intention for accuracy, be indulgent. Whatever things are difficult of access for the mind to contemplate are troublesome to interpret and do not have an easy grip to seize them. Yet, we have much hope that, through the prayers of your reverence, Christ guides us in this also, he who

---

1. For the critical text of this letter see Schwartz, *ACO* 1.1.4 pp. 40–48. Geerard numbers this letter 5341 in *CPG*. See also Wickham, *Select Letters*, 34–61.
2. Acacius, Bishop of Scythopolis.

"removes the depths from the darkness,"[3] "gives sight to the blind,"[4] and "grants speech,"[5] as it is written.

(3) Accordingly, it is written in Leviticus concerning the scapegoat, "and he shall take two male goats";[6] "and he shall set them before the Lord at the entrance of the Tent of Testimony and Aaron shall cast lots to determine which one is for the Lord and which for the emissary goat.[7] The goat, that is determined by lot for the Lord, Aaron shall bring in and offer up as a sin offering. But the goat determined by lot for the emissary goat, he shall set alive before the Lord so that with it he may make atonement by sending him off into the desert."[8] And after other matters, "Then he shall slaughter the people's sin-offering goat before the Lord and, bringing its blood inside the veil, he shall do with it as he did with the bullock's blood, sprinkling it upon the propitiatory and before it. Thus he will propitiate the sanctuary from the impieties of the sons of Israel and from their wrongdoings in all their sins. He shall do the same for the Tent of Testimony, which is set up among them in the midst of their uncleanness."[9] And these are the rites of the goat slaughtered and sanctifying the holy tent with his blood. Concerning the one living and the one sent out Scripture speaks again in this way, "And he shall bring forward the live goat. And Aaron shall lay both hands on the head of the live goat and shall confess over it all the transgressions, injustices and sins of the Israelites and put them on the head of the living goat, and he shall send it away into the desert by the hand of a man who is ready. And the goat will carry off on himself their

3. Jb 12.22.
4. Ps 145(146).8.
5. Ps 67(68).12.
6. Lv 16.5. This chapter of Leviticus describes the rites for the Day of Atonement.
7. See Lv 16.8, 10, 26. The ancients translated this word into Greek as: ʼαποπομπαῖος, the "escaping" or the "emissary goat." The Hebrew word, *Azazel*, is used only here in the Bible. It is perhaps a name for satan, and the goat used would then signify that the sins of the people are being sent back to the source of evil. Cf. R. J. Faley, *JBC* 4:34 and J. J. Castelot, *JBC* 76:157.
8. Lv 16.7–10.
9. Cf. Lv 16.15, 16.

iniquities to an isolated region, and he will send the goat away into the desert."[10] "All Scripture is inspired by God and useful."[11] Whatsoever God utters, this is in all aspects also conducive to salvation. And for those who are able to understand the power of the truth, its beauty comes to meet them after the manner of light and flashes upon their minds the knowledge of the mystery concerning Christ.

(4) To those who do not have a well-ordered mind, but, as it were, are still limp and play like children, to these, chosen subjects for speculation are under censure and sometimes indictment. I say these things regarding the writings of your reverence which have met with questioning. For perhaps some of those there thought that the first of the goats or bucks was allotted to God, who is over all things, as a dedication and a sacrifice, while the other one was sent into the desert to some abominable, wretched and unclean demon,[12] and this by the hand of a priest and as a result of a legal decree. From this point, therefore, the matter is simple-minded and ridiculous. And one might say to those who have accepted that this is so, "And how, indeed, was it not necessary to meditate somewhat about the following?" For how would he who is the fashioner of all things, who is beyond all thought and word, and alone is God and Lord by nature, endure admitting the apostate, satan, as a consort, as it were, of his power and glory? And we have heard him saying clearly through one of the holy prophets, "My glory I will give to no other."[13] But if the law enjoined through the all-wise Moses that it was necessary to sacrifice to him and to him alone whatever anyone wished to sacrifice, and if he who announced the law proclaimed that it was necessary that the glory most fitting to him and to him alone be assigned to unclean spirits, how is he not at variance with his own words? For what he told them not to do, he has enjoined that it be done.

---

10. Cf. Lv 16.20–22.

11. 2 Tm 3.16.

12. Evidently some of those under Acacius accepted *Azazel* in the text. See note 19. The problem is an ancient one. Cyril argued for a different meaning.

13. Is 42.8.

(5) But it is among the most exceedingly strange things to think that God, who exercises authority over all, pays no heed to the honor and glory due to him and wishes to fasten it to others, although he clearly says through Moses, "The Lord your God shall you worship and him only shall you serve";[14] and, "You shall have no other gods besides me."[15] Because of this, the divinely inspired Moses acted in accordance with the decrees from on high from God, and he says to those of the blood of Israel, "These are the statutes and decrees which you must be careful to observe in the land which the Lord, the God of your fathers, gives you to occupy, as long as you live on its soil. Destroy without fail every place on the high mountains, on the hills, and under every leafy tree where the nations you are to dispossess worship their gods. Tear down their altars, smash their sacred pillars, cut down their groves, destroy by fire the idols of their gods and stamp out the remembrance of them in any such place."[16]

(6) Then how was it likely that he, who gives commands that they be removed from the guile of the pagans to the light of the truth through Moses, and that they burn the idols to ashes along with their temples, and dig up their altars, and cut down the groves, so that no remnant of their abomination might remain behind, would share his glory with them, as I already said before, and come to this opinion so that he would order the Israelites to sacrifice to them the very animals allotted to him as an act of worship, by sending away one of the goats into the desert? He vehemently accused Israel for making a golden calf in the desert, saying to the divinely inspired Moses, "Get up, go down at once to your people, whom you brought out of the land of Egypt for they have fallen upon evil ways. They have made for themselves an idol."[17] He also is seen to have inflicted a keen punishment on those who took part in the sacrifice to Beelphegor when they involved themselves with Moabite women, being ensnared by their comeliness to apostasy, for large was the number of them who perished because

---

14. Mt 4.10; Dt 6.13.
15. Ex 20.3.

16. Cf. Dt 12.1–3.
17. Cf. Ex 32.7–9.

of this crime.[18] But in no small way would it have been a censure against the divine and faultless will, if, on the one hand, some fell and were destroyed for adoring other gods, but God himself, who was angry at the rebels, had enjoined that the depraved power opposed to him be deemed worthy of gifts, the power which perhaps some who, because the eyes in their minds within are blind, do not see the force of holy Scripture and would name *apopompaios*.[19] But we, dedicating our minds to divine inspiration, not carelessly or lazily but with precision and loving watchfulness, as far as and as much as possible, are very zealous in the love of hunting for the admirable beauty of the truth.

(7) Moreover, we say that the God of all, by promulgating the law to the ancients through Moses to overthrow the error of polytheism and to illumine those in darkness,[20] would never have endured becoming a way and a door, or rather a teacher of the need to honor the unclean demons. But, by deeply considering the matters in the divinely inspired Scriptures, we shall find the hidden truth. It would be fitting for us when looking into the dark shadows of the law to say what one of the holy prophets rightly said, "Who will be wise will understand these things; and who will be prudent will know them."[21] "For the law has but a shadow of the good things to come, and not the exact image of the objects,"[22] as it is written. Yet the shadows bring forth the truth, even if they are not at all the truth themselves. Because of this, the divinely inspired Moses placed a veil upon his face and spoke thus to the children of Israel,[23] all but shouting by this act that a person might behold the beauty of the utterances made through him, not in outwardly appearing figures, but in meditations hidden within us.[24]

(8) Come, therefore, by taking off the veil of the law and by

18. Cf. Nm 25.1–9.
19. That is, *Azazel*, in Hebrew, cf. note 12.
20. Lk 1.79; Mt 4.16; Is 9.1.
21. Hos 14.10.
22. Heb 10.1.
23. Cf. Ex 34.33–35; 2 Cor 3.13–17.
24. Cf. 2 Cor 4.3, 4, 18.

setting the face of Moses free of its coverings, let us behold the naked truth. He commanded that two he-goats be brought and two dice be marked for them, so that the one of the he-goats would be named the Lord's and the other named the scapegoat. Accordingly, the names for the he-goats are, the Lord's and the scapegoat. Through both of them the one and only Son and Lord Jesus Christ is signified. By attending to the accuracy of our meditations, as far as is possible, we shall tell how this is so. Accordingly, the goat, or the he-goat, or the kid was the sacrifice for sin according to the decision of the law, for the divinely inspired Scripture in very many places compares the just to sheep and the lover of iniquity to a goat. And for what sort of reason? Because the just man is full of glory unto virtue and for this he is fittingly considered fruitful. But the sheep bears wool, and so for this reason the just man is likened to a sheep, and very fittingly. But one would behold the soul of a sinner as naked and sterile and bereft of all good deeds. Therefore, the goat is the sign of that soul, for the animal is unproductive and lower in price than a sheep. For this reason, also, our Lord Jesus Christ says, "But when the Son of Man will sit on the throne of his glory; and he will set the sheep on his right hand, but the goats on his left."[25] To those on his right hand, since they have the fruits of justice, he delivers the kingdom prepared for them, but to those on his left hand, fire and punishment, and he will inflict the penalties proper to the devil.

(9) Accordingly, the kid was sacrificed for sin and you will understand this since the law clearly says, "If a prince shall sin and shall do so inadvertently, one of the things which shall not be done from all the commandments of the Lord, his God, and shall sin and shall err and the sin which he committed shall in itself be known to him, he shall bring as his offering from his goats an unblemished male goat."[26] And elsewhere, the God of all himself said concerning those to whom the priesthood was allotted according to the law, "They feed on the sin of my

25. Cf. Mt 25.31–33.
26. Lv 4.22, 23.

people,"[27] that is, on the sacrifices for sins. For the share and heritage of the priests is the portion due to the Lord, according to Scripture.[28]

(10) Thus Christ became a victim "for our sins according to the Scriptures."[29] For this reason, we say that he was named sin; wherefore, the all-wise Paul writes, "For our sakes he made him to be sin who knew nothing of sin,"[30] that is to say, God the Father. For we do not say that Christ became a sinner, far from it, but being just, or rather in actuality justice, for he did not know sin, the Father made him a victim for the sins of the world. "He was counted among the wicked,"[31] having endured a condemnation most suitable for the wicked. And the divinely inspired prophet Isaiah will also vouch for this, saying, "We had all gone astray like sheep, each following his own way, but the Lord laid upon him the guilt of us all," "yet it was on our behalf he suffers," "and by his stripes we were healed."[32] The all-wise Peter writes, "he bore our sins in his body upon the tree."[33]

(11) Therefore, the lot of the necessary endurance of death hung over those on the earth through the transgression in Adam and through sin reigning from him until us.[34] But the Word of God the Father, being generous in clemency and love of men, became flesh, that is, man, in the form of us who are under sin, and he endured our lot. For as the very excellent Paul writes, "By the grace of God he tasted death for all,"[35] and he made his life be an exchange for the life of all. One died for all, in order that we all might live to God sanctified and brought to life through his blood,[36] "justified as a gift by his grace."[37] For as the blessed evangelist John says, "The blood of Jesus Christ cleanses us from all sin."[38]

(12) The name, therefore, of the immolated goat was the Lord's, and he received his allotted immolation, a holy sac-

27. Hos 4.8.
28. Cf. Dt 18.1–3.
29. 1 Cor 15.3; Is 53.4–6.
30. 2 Cor 5.21.
31. Is 53.12.
32. Is 53.6, 4, 5.

33. 1 Pt 2.24.
34. Cf. Rom 5.12–17.
35. Heb 2.9.
36. Cf. Rom 5.12–21.
37. Rom 3.24.
38. 1 Jn 1.7.

rifice, and it was sacred as a sign of Christ who did not die for himself but for us, as I said, and sanctified the church with his blood. Moses says, "He shall slaughter the male goat, the one for sin, the one for the people, before the Lord and shall bring its blood inside the veil, and shall sprinkle it upon the propitiatory and before the propitiatory, and he shall cleanse the sanctuary from the defilements of the sons of Israel and from their transgressions on account of all their sins. And he shall do the same for the Tent of Testimony which is set up among them in the midst of their uncleanness."[39] "For Christ entered into the Holy of Holies, not by virtue of blood of goats and calves, but by virtue of his own blood, having obtained eternal redemption"[40] and sanctifying, as I said, the truer tent, that is, the church and all those in it. Therefore, the divinely inspired Paul once wrote, "and so Jesus also, that he might sanctify the people by his blood, suffered outside the gate."[41] And once again, "Be you, therefore, imitators of God, as very dear children and walk in love, as Christ also loved us and delivered himself up for us an offering and a sacrifice to God to ascend in fragrant odor."[42] Except for the destruction of death and sin we must perceive the Emmanuel in the slaughtered goat by his death in the flesh, for he was "free among the dead,"[43] that is, untainted by sins and not subject to the penalty of death together with us.

(13) Let us see him in the other living goat sent away, and in his suffering as man, but not suffering as God, and in his dying in the flesh, but being greater than death, and in not remaining, according to the madness of the Jews, in the tomb as we do, and not being held fast by the gates of the underworld together with the other dead. For as his disciple says, "You will not abandon my soul to the underworld, nor will you suffer your holy one to see corruption."[44] For he rose again, despoiling death and "saying to the prisoners: Come out, to those in darkness: Show yourselves,"[45] and he ascended to his Father

39. Lv 16.15, 16.
40. Heb 9.12.
41. Heb 13.12.
42. Eph 5.1, 2; cf. Ex 29.18.

43. Cf. Ps 87.5.
44. Ps 15.10; Acts 2.27.
45. Is 49.9.

above in the heavens to a position inaccessible to men, having taken upon himself our sins and being the propitiation for them. Hence, the divinely inspired John writes to those who believe in him, "My dear children, these things I write to you in order that you may not sin. But if anyone sins, we have an advocate with the Father, Jesus Christ the just; and he is a propitiation for our sins, not for ours only, but also for those of the whole world."[46]

(14) But I think it is necessary to make a comparison of the Scriptures as a reminder to my listeners.[47] And the Scriptures are as follows, "And he shall bring forward the living male goat, and Aaron shall place his hands upon the living male goat. And he shall confess over it all the transgressions of the sons of Israel and all their wrongdoings and put them on the head of the living goat, and he shall send it forth into the desert in the hand of a man who is ready."[48] Consider, therefore, how he calls the second goat the living one, although the first goat was sacrificed.[49] For, as I said, the one and only Son and Lord, Jesus Christ, was depicted in both as in suffering in his own flesh, and beyond suffering, as in death and above death. For the Word of God lived, even though his holy flesh tasted death, and the Word of God remained impassible, although he made his own the suffering of his own body and took it upon himself.

(15) One might see that this is a deep and great mystery and one delineated for us in a different way in Leviticus. For the law through Moses pronounces that the leper has been defiled, and has enjoined that he be sent forth from the encampment as unclean. But if it should happen that his disease has come to an end, then, indeed, then it bids that he be admitted. And moreover, it says:

This is the law of the leper on whatever day he is cleansed; he shall also be brought to the priest, who is to go outside the

46. 1 Jn 2.1, 2.
47. From this, we conclude that Cyril expected his letter to be read aloud to a group.
48. Cf. Lv 16.20–22.
49. The second goat was different. It was not to be sacrificed. It was left alive.

camp to examine him. And behold the sore of leprosy has healed in the leper and the priest shall command and they shall take for the man who is to be purified two live, clean birds. The priest shall command and they shall slay one of the birds over an earthen vessel with living water in it. And he shall take the living bird, and shall dip it in the blood of the bird that was slain over the living water and then sprinkle seven times the man to be purified from his leprosy, and he shall be clean, and he shall send the living bird out in the plain.[50]

There are two birds, therefore, and pure ones, that is, clean and having no fault, I mean according to the law. And the one was sacrificed over the living water, but the other, remaining free of being slain and then dipped in the blood of the one killed and in the living water, was sent forth in the exact same way as the goat is sent forth into the desert.

(16) And in this, a type would be indicated and, again, the great and august mystery of our Savior. For he was from above, that is, from his Father, and the Word from heaven. In this, and very rightly, he is likened to the bird. And in the Incarnation he came among us in our likeness and "took the form of a slave."[51] And yet he was from above. And he said, clearly speaking to the Jews, "You are from below, I am from above. I am not of this world";[52] and again, "No one has ascended into heaven except him who has descended from heaven: the Son of Man."[53] As I said just recently, even after he was made flesh, that is, perfect man, he was not of earth or of dust as we are, but heavenly and above the world, just as in our thoughts God is conceived to be. Yet, it is possible to see him in the birds just as in the goats, suffering in his flesh according to the Scriptures, but remaining also beyond suffering, and dying as man, but living as God, for the Word was life.[54] And his all-wise disciple said that he "was put to death indeed in the flesh, but he was brought to life in the spirit."[55]

(17) Yet, even if he suffered death in his own nature, the

50. Lv 14.2–7.
51. Cf. Phil 2.6, 7.
52. Jn 8.23.
53. Jn 3.13.
54. Cf. Jn 1.4.
55. 1 Pt 3.18.

Word has no share in death, but made his own the suffering of his own flesh, as I already said before. For the living bird was dipped in the blood of the one slain, having been stained with its blood, and all but took part in its suffering and was sent into the desert. The only begotten Word of God ascended in the heavens with his flesh united to him, and this was a new sight in the heavens. The multitude of holy angels was astounded seeing the king of glory and the Lord of hosts in the form like unto us. And they said, "Who is this that comes from Edom (that is, from earth),[56] in crimsoned garments, from Bosor."[57] But Bosor is interpreted flesh or anguish and affliction. Then the angels asked this, "What are these wounds in the middle of your hands?" And he said to them, "With these I was wounded in the house of my beloved."[58] For just as to Thomas, who doubted and did so very much in accordance with the economy of salvation after the Resurrection from the dead, he showed his hands and in them the marks of the nails, and ordered Thomas to feel the opening in his side,[59] so, also, after he was in heaven, he assured the holy angels that his beloved Israel was justly cast out and utterly lost from their friendship. For this reason, he showed his garment stained with blood and the wounds in his hands, not because he had wounds incapable of being cast aside, for, when he rose from the dead, he put off corruption and with it all that is from it, but, as I said, "in order that through the church there be made known to the principalities and the powers in the heavens the manifold wisdom of God according to his eternal plan which he accomplished in Christ."[60] For the most holy Paul writes thus to some. Therefore, just as in the goats the mystery of Christ is wisely depicted, so is it also in the small birds.

(18) But perhaps someone will say, "How, then, do you say that the Son and Lord, Jesus Christ, is one and the same, although two goats have been mentioned, and two birds? Or might the law, not obscurely undoubtedly, show that there are

56. This is Cyril's interpretation.   59. Cf. Jn 20.26–28.
57. Cf. Is 63.1.   60. Eph 3.10, 11.
58. Zec 13.6.

in some way entirely two sons and christs?" And some have already descended to such a degree of impiety as to think and say that the Word of God the Father is one Christ taken separately and the other one is of the seed of David. But we say to those who entertain thoughts that this is so out of ignorance, and the divinely inspired Paul writes, "one Lord, one faith, one baptism."[61] So if they say two sons, there would in all events be two lords, and two faiths, and two baptisms.

(19) Therefore, Paul, who had Christ speaking in him,[62] as he said, was telling lies! But such is not the case; heaven forbid! Therefore, there is one Lord and one faith, and one baptism. For we believe in one Lord, Jesus Christ, that is, the only begotten Word of God made man and incarnate. Because of this, also, "we have been baptized into his death,"[63] and we know that he alone is Lord as God, not taking him apart as man and God, but, as I said, maintaining that the Word of God the Father himself became man while remaining God, for he is immutable and unchangeable according to nature as God.

(20) Then, if those on the opposite side say that there are two sons, one taken separately of the seed of David, and the other, again separately the Word of God the Father, let them state whether or not the Word of God the Father, is better by nature than the one of the seed of David, and by incomparable differences. For what is the nature of man compared to the divine and supreme? But I think they will say, and not willingly, that the Word of God the Father is better by nature. Then, what will we do, seeing that the two goats are not of different natures to each other, but rather similar in species and differing in no way from each other insofar as being what they are is concerned? And the same reasoning would occur also in the case of the two birds. They should concede, since the goats are similar in species, or the birds are similar in species, that the Word of God is no different from man. But they will not agree, as I think, to such reasoning, for there is the greatest difference between divinity and humanity.

61. Eph 4.5.
62. Cf. 2 Cor 13.3.
63. Rom 6.3.

(21) We should allow the examples to be considered according to the explanation suited to them. For the examples are very much less than the truth and are incomplete indications of the things signified. But we say that the law was a shadow and a type,[64] and like unto a picture set as a thing to be viewed before those watching reality. But the silhouettes of artists' skill are the first elements of the lines in pictures, and, if the brightness of the colors is added to these, the beauty of the picture flashes forth. It was fitting, therefore, that the law given through Moses, since its intention was to delineate the mystery of Christ, should not present him by one of the goats or one of the birds, dying and living at the same time, lest the deed might seem to be somehow a wonder-working show, but it regards him in one of them as suffering his immolation, and presents him in the other as living and having been set free.

(22) But to show that my reasoning on this matter is not going beyond probability, I think it will be necessary to add another image to those which I have mentioned. Accordingly, it is written in the book concerning creation:

> And after these events God put Abraham to a test. He said to him, "Abraham, Abraham." He answered, "Here I am." God said, "Take your dear son Isaac whom you have loved and go into the high country and there offer him as a holocaust on the hill which I tell you." Early in the morning Abraham harnassed his ass, took with him two of his servants, and his son Isaac, and cut wood for the holocaust. Then he came to the place that God told him on the third day. He looked up and saw the place at a distance. He said to his servants, "Stay here with the ass while the boy and I go there to worship, then we shall come back to you." He took the wood for the holocaust and put it upon his son Isaac while he himself carried the fire and the knife. And the two set out together.[65]

And after other verses, "Abraham built an altar of sacrifice there and arranged the wood on it. Then he bound his son

64. Cf. Heb 10.1.
65. Gn 22.1–6.

Isaac and laid him on the wood upon an altar of sacrifice. Abraham stretched out his hand to take the knife to sacrifice his son."[66] Accordingly, if someone of us desired to see the story of Abraham portrayed in a picture, how would the painter represent him? Would he do it in a single painting showing him doing all the things mentioned,[67] or in successive pictures and distinctively, or in different images, but most often Abraham himself, for example, in one picture sitting on his donkey taking his son along and followed by his servants; in another one, again, with the donkey staying behind down below along with the servants, and Isaac being burdened with the wood while Abraham holds in his hands the knife and the fire; and, indeed, in a different painting, Abraham again in a different pose after he has bound the youth upon the wood and his right hand is armed with a sword in order that he might start the sacrifice? But this would not be a different Abraham each time, although he is seen most of the time in a different pose, but would be the same man in every instance with the skill of the artist continually disposing him according to the needs of the subject matter. For it would not be likely or at any rate probable that one would see him doing all the actions mentioned in a single painting.

(23) Accordingly, the law was a picture and, in the law, the types of things were fertile with the truth, with the result that even if the precept introduced two goats to illustrate the mystery of Christ and even if there were two birds, he in both was one, both in suffering and beyond suffering, and in death and over death and ascending in the heavens, the first-fruits of humanity,[68] as it were, thereafter restored unto incorruption.

(24) For he restored for us the pathway upward and we will follow him in due season, for he says, "I go to prepare a place for you and I am coming again and I will take you to myself, that where I am, there you also may be with me."[69] We have these true hopes.

66. Gn 22.9, 10.
67. This is the narrative style of ancient paintings.
68. Cf. 1 Cor 15.20.
69. Jn 14.2, 3.

(25) Therefore, I have written the things which I knew, but it is your reverence's part to bring to bear on what I have written a rather precise examination, in order that, if it should happen that something of an improvement might be discovered, it might benefit both us and the people here. For Christ is the one who reveals profound and hidden things[70] and implants understanding in our hearts. For in him and with him "are hidden all the treasures of wisdom and knowledge."[71] Through him and with him may there be glory and power to God the Father with the Holy Spirit unto ages of ages. Amen.

70. Cf. Mt 11.25–27.
71. Col 2.3.

LETTER 42

To Rufus, Bishop of Thessalonica.[1]

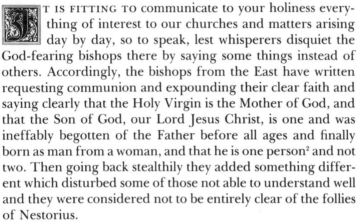T IS FITTING TO communicate to your holiness every-
thing of interest to our churches and matters arising
day by day, so to speak, lest whisperers disquiet the
God-fearing bishops there by saying some things instead of
others. Accordingly, the bishops from the East have written
requesting communion and expounding their clear faith and
saying clearly that the Holy Virgin is the Mother of God, and
that the Son of God, our Lord Jesus Christ, is one and was
ineffably begotten of the Father before all ages and finally
born as man from a woman, and that he is one person[2] and not
two. Then going back stealthily they added something different which disturbed some of those not able to understand well
and they were considered not to be entirely clear of the follies
of Nestorius.

(2) My lord Acacius, the God-fearing Bishop of Melitene,
wrote about these things to me. And it was necessary to com-
pose a rather long letter and to clarify the statements of the
bishops from the East at which some had been scandalized.
Hence I have sent a copy of the letter, so that if some of those
there also are found to be suffering from the same problem, by
looking into my letter they would have the means to know the
truth. Yet I know that I have done this superfluously since your
excellency is fully capable of being able to explain everything
and confer the benefit of your knowledge upon those who
have been overcome by ignorance.

1. For the critical text of this letter see E. Schwartz, *Codex vaticanus gr. 1431:
Eine antichalkedonische Sammlung aus der Zeit Kaiser Zenos* in *Abhandlungen der
Bayerischen Akademie der Wissenschaften philosophisch-philologische und historische
Klasse*, no. 6 (Munich, 1927), 32:19. Geerard numbers this letter 5342 in *CPG*.
2. Cf. Letter 40, note 30.

LETTER 43

To Rufus of Thessalonica.[1]

ECAUSE OF THE PEACE of the churches and the fact that they are not pulled asunder in dissensions, considerations are not unprofitable. For it is likely that those who have not been received into communion may come to some other opinion ill-advisedly because of lack of care. For heresies are brought forth and schisms follow or else uninterrupted disorders, since they are not accustomed to endure great censure.

(2) In view of this I was very much pleased when the bishops from the East pursued and sought communion with us and especially because it also happened opportunely since our most pious and most God-loving ruler wrote about this matter. For the unanimity of the churches has been an inevitable care for his serenity. And when you consider this, let your excellency be inclined to do whatever is fitting and looks to the benefit of the churches of God there.

(3) Accordingly, I have written concerning the matter in consideration of the advantages and it is the part of your excellency to attempt the accomplishment. For it is better to receive back those who repent rather than that they be added in utter shamelessness to the group of those who choose to think as Nestorius does. And, although you are all-wise and all-perfect,[2] since you commanded me to send some one of my works and since you tolerate my babbling tongue, I dared to

1. For the critical text of this letter see Schwartz, *Codex vaticanus gr. 1431*, 19–20, Geerard numbers this letter 5343 in *CPG*.
2. These are the most extreme of the courtly superlatives in the letters of Cyril.

send so far four books containing a long discussion concerning the economy of salvation of our Savior from passages of the Old Testament. But I included also what I have written against the blasphemies of Nestorius, and your excellency is able enough in this matter to aid both us and all those there, since I was led to this action out of charity. After you have read and corrected them, if anything has been overlooked, deign to show them to the rest of the brethren. The books are as follows: one book *On Genesis*, two books *Concerning Worship in Spirit and in Truth*, the chapters against the writing of Theodoret and Andrew, and one book on the Incarnation, *Against the Blasphemies of Nestorius.*[3]

3. Cf. Quasten 3.120–127 for a description of these works.

LETTER 44

A Memorandum to Eulogius, the priest, who is staying at Constantinople, from the most holy bishop Cyril. Cyril, Bishop of Alexandria, to Eulogius. Greetings.[1]

OME ATTACK THE exposition of faith which those from the East have made and ask, "For what reason did the Bishop of Alexandria endure or even praise those who say that there are two natures?" Those who hold the same teachings as Nestorius say that he thinks the same thing too, snatching to their side those who do not understand precision. But it is necessary to say the following to those who are accusing me, namely, that it is not necessary to flee and avoid everything which heretics say, for they confess many of the things which we confess. For example, when the Arians say that the Father is the creator and Lord of all, does it follow that we avoid such confessions? Thus also is the case of Nestorius even if he says there are two natures signifying the difference of the flesh and the Word of God, for the nature of the Word is one nature and the nature of his flesh is another, but Nestorius does not any longer confess the union as we do.

(2) For we, when asserting their union, confess one Christ, one Son, the one and same Lord, and finally we confess the one incarnate *phusis* of God.[2] It is possible to say something such as this about any ordinary man, for he is of different natures, both of the body, I say, and of the soul. Both reason and speculation know the difference, but when combined then we

---

1. For the critical text of this letter see Schwartz, *ACO* 1.1.4 pp. 35–37. Geerard numbers this letter 5344 in *CPG*. See also Ebied-Wickham, *Unpublished Syriac Letters*, 44–46, and Wickham, *Select Letters*, 62–69.
2. Cf. Letter 40, note 22.

get one human *phusis*. Hence knowing the difference of the natures is not cutting the one Christ into two.

(3) But since all the bishops from the East think that we, who are orthodox, follow the opinions of Apollinaris and think that a mixture or a confusion took place, for such are the words which they have used, as if the Word of God had changed over into the nature of flesh, and his flesh had turned into the nature of divinity, we have yielded to them, not so far as to divide into two the one Son, far from it, but only to confess that neither a mixture nor a confusion took place, but the flesh was flesh as taken from a woman, and the Word as begotten of the Father was the Word, yet the Christ, Son and Lord, is one according to the saying of John, "The Word was made flesh,"[3] and to prepare them to pay heed to the reading of the letter of our blessed father, Athanasius.[4]

(4) Because in his time some were contending and saying that God the Word from his own nature fashioned a body for himself, he stoutly insisted to and fro that his body was not consubstantial to the Word. But if it is not consubstantial, then there is one nature and a completely other nature from which two the one and only Son is known to be. And let those accusing me not be ignorant of this, namely, that when there is mention of a union, it does not signify the coming together of one thing, but of either two or more which are also different from each other according to nature. If, then, we speak of a union we are confessing a union of flesh animated with a rational soul and the Word, and those who speak of two natures are thinking thus also.

(5) Yet once we confess the union, those things which have been united are no longer separate from each other, but then there is one Son, and his *phusis*[5] is one as the Word made flesh. The bishops from the East confess these doctrines, even though they are somewhat obscure concerning the expres-

---

3. Jn 1.14.
4. The letter to Epictetus of Corinth. Cf. Letter 40.
5. Cf. Letter 40, note 22.

sion.[6] For since they confess that the only begotten Word begotten of God the Father was himself also begotten of a woman according to flesh, that the Holy Virgin is the Mother of God, that his person is one, and that there are not two sons, or two christs, but one, how do they agree with the teachings of Nestorius?

(6) For Nestorius in his expositions pretends to say that the Son is one and the Lord is one but he refers the sonship and the lordship only to the Word of God, but when he comes to the dispensation of the Incarnation, again he says that the man born of woman is separately another Lord conjoined to the first by worthiness or equality of honor. But how is saying that in this way God the Word is named Christ because he has the conjoining with Christ not clearly stating that there are two christs, if a christ has a conjoining with a christ as one with another? But the bishops from the East have said no such thing; they only separate the sayings.[7]

(7) And they separate them in this manner. Some are proper to his divinity, others are human, and others have a position in common as being both proper to his divinity and his humanity. Yet they are sayings concerning him, one and the same, and not as Nestorius ascribes some to God the Word taken separately, and others to him born of woman as to another son. For it is one thing to know the difference of the sayings and another to distribute them to two persons as if to one and then to another.

(8) But the letter to Acacius,[8] especially the one which has as its beginning, "Addressing one another is a sweet thing for brothers and admirable" contains a fine answer on all these matters. And you have very many letters in your chest, which you ought to give out zealously, and offer also to the most

6. This is ironic, looking back on events from our standpoint. Actually the bishops of the East were more exact in expression for they used πρόσωπον not φύσις. Cyril here defends them. Their term was not well accepted in some circles.

7. The sayings in the Gospels and apostolic writings by Christ and about him. Cf. Letter 40, notes 19 and 21.

8. Letter 40.

illustrious prefect the two books sent from me, the first being *Against the Blasphemies of Nestorius,*[9] the second containing the conciliar acts against Nestorius and his adherents, and the refutations written by me against those who wrote against the propositions. These are two bishops, Andrew and Theodoret.[10] And the same book at the end contains concise expositions about the dispensations concerning Christ, very fine and useful. Offer to him likewise, of those on parchment, five letters; first the letter of our blessed father Athanasius to Epictetus,[11] and second the letter to John from us,[12] and two letters to Nestorius, one short letter and one long letter,[13] and finally the letter to Acacius,[14] for he requested these from us.

9. Composed in 430. See Quasten 3.126.
10. Ibid., 127. Wickham (cf. note 1 supra) identifies the prefect as Chryseros, the eunuch who is also mentioned in Letter 96.

11. Quasten 3.59.	13. Possibly Letter 2 or 4 and 17.
12. Possibly Letter 39.	14. Possibly Letter 33.

LETTER 45

Cyril, to Succensus, most blessed Bishop of Diocaesarea in Isauria.[1]

READ THE MEMORANDUM sent by your holiness and I was exceedingly pleased because, although you are able to help both us and others from your very great love of wisdom, yet you deign to urge us to write about what we hold in our own mind and what we understand you think also. Accordingly, concerning the dispensation of our Savior we think as the holy Fathers before us thought also. For, when reading their works, we put their thought in such order as to follow after them and to introduce nothing strange to the orthodoxy of their teachings.

(2) But since your excellency is inquiring whether it is proper to speak of two natures in Christ or not, I thought I ought to speak on this matter. A certain Diodore,[2] a sometime contender of the Holy Spirit,[3] as they say, at one time was in communion with the church of the true faith.[4] After he had put aside, as he thought, the blot of the Macedonian heresy,[5] he fell into another sickness. For he thought and he wrote that there is one son separately begotten of the seed of David from the Holy Virgin, the Mother of God, and again another Son begotten

1. For the critical text of this letter see Schwartz, *ACO* 1.1.6 pp. 151–157. Geerard numbers this letter 5345 in *CPG*. See also Ebied-Wickham, *Unpublished Syriac Letter*, 32–38, and Wickham, *Select Letters*, 70–83.

2. Diodore of Tarsus against whom Cyril wrote a tractate, cf. Quasten 3.128, 397–401.

3. Gregory of Nyssa wrote against this sect, cf. Quasten 3.259.

4. Diodore died before 394, a member of the true church. Cyril accused him of Nestorianism as early as 438, and later Diodore's writings were condemned by a synod at Constantinople in 499.

5. This sect called the "contenders against the Spirit" was led by Macedonius, Bishop of Constantinople, deposed in 360.

separately, the Word of God the Father. As if concealing the wolf in a fleece of a sheep,[6] he pretended to say that there is one Christ, by referring the name Christ just to the only begotten Son, the Word begotten of God the Father, since he allots the name to him in the order of grace, as he says himself, and he calls him the son of the seed of David as one united, he says, to the one who is truly the Son, united, however, not as we glorify him, but only according to dignity and according to authority and according to equality of honor.

(3) Nestorius became the disciple of this Diodore, and then with mind darkened by his books he pretends to confess one Christ, Son and Lord, but he himself also divides the one into two, saying that the undivided man was connected to God the Word by the same name, by the same honor, and by dignity. And so he separates the sayings made about Christ in the evangelical and apostolic proclamations and says that some ought to be attributed to the man, obviously the statements proper to the humanity, and others alone are suited to God the Word, obviously those proper to divinity. And since in many places he divides and successively regards the one begotten from the Holy Virgin as man separately, and likewise separately and successively the Son, the Word of God the Father, for this reason he says that the Holy Virgin is not the Mother of God, but rather the mother of a man.[7]

(4) But we are not disposed to hold these as true, but we were taught according to the divine Scripture and the holy Fathers and we confess that one Son and Christ and Lord, that is, the Word of God the Father, was begotten of him before ages in a divinely fitting and ineffable manner and that in recent ages of time the same Son was begotten for us according to the flesh from the Holy Virgin, and since she gave birth to God made man and made flesh, for this reason we also call her the Mother of God. Therefore there is one Son, "one Lord Jesus Christ"[8] both before his Incarnation and after his In-

---

6. Cf. Mt 7.15.
7. The Greek is ανθρωποτόκος.
8. 1 Cor 8.6. Cf. Wolfson, *Philosophy of the Fathers*, 1:408.

carnation. For there was not one Son, the Word of God the Father, and again another one of the Holy Virgin, but our belief is that he is the same who was before ages and was begotten according to flesh of a woman, not that his divinity received a beginning unto existence or that his existence was summoned unto a beginning through the Holy Virgin, but rather, as I said, that the Word, who was before ages, is said to have been begotten from her according to the flesh. For his flesh was his own, just as by all means each one of us has his own body.

(5) But since some people bind upon us the opinions of Apollinaris and say, "If you speak of one Son according to a perfect and commingled union, who is the Word of God the Father made man and incarnate, at once without doubt you seem to think and you knew you thought that a mixture, or a blending, or a confusion of the Word took place with his body, or else a change of his body into the nature of divinity." For this reason and very wisely we say in answer to this calumny that the Word of God the Father incomprehensibly and in a manner which cannot be expressed united to himself a body animated by a rational soul and came forth a man from a woman, having become like unto us, not by a change of his nature but rather by the goodwill of the dispensation of his Incarnation. For he chose to become man without losing what he was as God by nature. But even if he descended unto the limitations which we have and has possessed "the form of a slave,"[9] although being so, he remained in the preeminence of his divinity and in his natural lordship.

(6) Accordingly when we assert the union of the Word of God the Father to his holy body which has a rational soul, a union which is ineffable and beyond thought and which took place without blending, without change, without alteration, we confess one Christ, Son and Lord, the Word of God the Father, the same God and man, not one and another, but one and the same, being, and known to be, God and man. Therefore sometimes he speaks as man according to the dispensation and

9. Phil 2.7.

according to his humanity, and sometimes as God he makes statements by the authority of his divinity. And we make the following assertions also. While skillfully examining the manner of his dispensation with flesh and finely probing the mystery, we see that the Word of God the Father was made man and was made flesh and that he has not fashioned that holy body from his divine nature but rather took it from the Virgin Mary. Since how did he become man, if he has not possessed a body like ours? Considering, therefore, as I said, the manner of his Incarnation we see that his two natures came together with each other in an indissoluble union, without blending and without change, for his flesh is flesh and not divinity, even though his flesh became the flesh of God, and likewise the Word also is God and not flesh, even though he made the flesh his own according to the dispensation. Therefore, whenever we have these thoughts in no way do we harm the joining into a unity by saying that he was of two natures, but after the union we do not separate the natures from one another, nor do we cut the one and indivisible Son into two sons, but we say that there is one Son, and as the holy Fathers have said,[10] that there is one *phusis* of the Word [of God] made flesh.[11]

(7) Therefore, as far as concerns our understanding and only the contemplation by the eyes of the soul in what manner the only begotten became man, we say that there are two natures which are united, but that Christ the Son and Lord is one, the Word of God the Father made man and incarnate. And, if it seems best, let us accept as an example the composition in our own selves by which we are men. For we are composed of soul and body and we see two natures, the one being the nature of the body and the other the nature of the soul, but there is one from both in unity, a man. And because man is composed of two natures, this does not make two men be one, but one and the same man through the composition, as I said, of soul and body. For if we should deny that the one and only Christ is from two different natures, and that he is indi-

10. Cf. Quasten 3.140.
11. This is the first instance of the famous formula in the letters. Here *phusis* means "person" to Cyril, cf. Letter 40, note 22.

visible after the union, those who are fighting against the true faith will say, "If the whole[12] is one *phusis*, how was he made man or what kind of body did he make his own?"

(8) But since I found in the Memorandum a certain suggestion of such an expression, to the effect that after the Resurrection the holy body of Christ, the Savior of us all, has changed into divinity so that the whole is only divinity, I thought it necessary to speak against this also. The blessed Paul writes somewhere when explaining the causes of the Incarnation of the only begotten Son of God: "For what was impossible to the law, in that it was weak because of the flesh, God has made good; by sending his Son in the likeness of sinful flesh as a sin-offering, he has condemned sin in the flesh, in order that the justification of the law might be fulfilled in us, who walk not according to the flesh but according to the Spirit."[13] And again somewhere:

> Since therefore the children share in blood and flesh, so he in like manner has shared in these; that through death he might destroy him who had the power of death, that is, the devil; and might deliver them, who throughout their lives were kept in servitude by the fear of death. For, of course, it is not angels that he is succoring, but he is succoring the offspring of Abraham. Wherefore it was right that he should in all things be made like unto his brethren.[14]

(9) Therefore we say that, since from the transgression of Adam human nature suffered corruption and since our intellect within us is tyrannized by the pleasures of the flesh or by the inborn motions of the flesh, it became necessary for the salvation of us who are upon the earth that the Word of God be made man in order that he might make his own the flesh of man although it was subject to corruption and sick with the love of pleasure. Since he is life and life-giver, he would destroy the corruption in the flesh and rebuke its inborn motions, plainly those which tend toward love of pleasure. For thus it

---

12. That is, the whole Christ after the Incarnation.
13. Rom 8.3, 4.
14. Heb 2.14–17.

was possible that the sin in our flesh be killed. We recalled also
that the blessed Paul called this inborn motion in us the "law of
sin."[15] Wherefore since human flesh became the Word's own,
the subjection to corruption has come to an end, and since as
God, he who made it his own and proclaimed it as his own "did
not know sin,"[16] as I said, he also put an end to the sickness of
loving pleasure. And the only begotten Word of God has not
corrected this for himself, for he is what he always is, but
obviously for us. For even if we have been subject to evil from
the transgression of Adam, by all means there will come upon
us also the good things of Christ, which are immortality and
the death of sin.

(10) Accordingly he became man, and did not assume a
man, as it seems to Nestorius. And in order that it might be
believed that he became man even though he remained what
he was, God by nature obviously, therefore it is reported that
he was hungry, and was weary from the journey, and endured
sleep, and trouble, and pain, and the other human blameless
experiences.

(11) And again, in order that he might give assurance to
those seeing him that in addition to being man he is also true
God, he worked signs of his divinity by rebuking the waves, by
raising the dead, and performing other marvelous deeds. And
he endured the cross also in order that by suffering death in his
flesh and not in the nature of his divinity he might become "the
first-born from the dead"[17] and might open up the road to
immortality for the nature of man and by despoiling Hades
might free the souls confined there.

(12) After the Resurrection it was the same body which had
suffered except it no longer had the human infirmities in it.
For we assert that it was no longer receptive of hunger, or of
weariness, or of anything else of such a kind, but was thereafter
incorruptible, and not only this but also life-giving, for it is the
body of life, that is, the body of the only begotten, for it has
been made resplendent with the glory most proper to his

15. Rom 7.25.
16. Cf. 1 Pt 2.22, Is 53.9, 1 Jn 3.5, 2 Cor 5.21, Jn 8.46.
17. Col 1.18.

divinity and is known to be the body of God. Therefore, even if some might say that it is divine, just as, of course, it is the human body of a man, he would not err from proper reasoning. Whence I think that the very wise Paul said, "And even though we have known Christ according to the flesh, yet now we know him so no longer."[18] For being God's own body, as I said, it transcends all human bodies.

(13) But it is not admissible that a body from earth underwent a change into the nature of divinity, for it is impossible, and, if we admit it, we are dishonoring divinity as something coming into being and as adding to itself something which was not proper to it according to nature. For as a statement of absurdity it is the same thing to say that the body was transformed into the nature of divinity, and to say this, that the Word was transformed into the nature of flesh, by saying that the divinity had changed itself into the nature of flesh. And just as the latter is impossible, for he is unchanged and unaltered, so also is the former impossible. For it is unattainable that any creature change into the essence or nature of divinity, and flesh is a creature. Therefore, on the one hand, we say that the body of Christ is divine, since it is the body of God, and we say that it is resplendent with ineffable glory, incorruptible, holy and life-giving, but, on the other hand, none of the holy Fathers has either thought or said that it was changed into the nature of divinity, nor are we of this opinion either.

(14) Let your holiness be not ignorant also of this, that our father Athanasius, of happy memory, who was once Bishop of Alexandria, because some persons were disturbed at that time, wrote a letter to Epictetus, the Bishop of Corinth, full of true doctrine. But since Nestorius was refuted by it, and since those who concurred in the true faith after reading it and taking proofs from it were putting to shame those who wished to think as he did, they perpetrated a wretched thing, and one worthy of their heretical impiety. For after they corrupted the letter by having taken out some things and having inserted others, they have published it, so that our glorious father

18. 2 Cor 5.16.

seems to agree with what Nestorius thinks and those with him. Therefore, lest some might show the corrupt version of it there also, it was necessary to take a copy from those which we have and send it to your reverence.[19]

(15) For, in truth, the most pious and most God-fearing Bishop of Emesa, Paul, after arriving in Alexandria, brought up a discussion concerning this, and the copy of the letter which he brought was found to have been corrupted and falsified by the heretics, so that he asked that a copy of those which we have be sent to Antioch and we have sent it. And following in every way the true doctrines of the holy Fathers we have composed a book against the teachings of Nestorius, and another one, too, since some were slandering the meaning of the propositions,[20] and I sent these to your reverence so that if there might be some of our brethren, like unto us in faith and in soul, but carried away by the follies of some people and thinking that we have changed in what was said against Nestorius, they might be refuted by the reading of these and learn that we well and rightly reproved him as one wandering from truth. And now we are no less devoted to fighting his blasphemies everywhere. And your excellency, being able to understand these greater matters, will be of aid to us both by writing and by praying for us.

19. Cf. Letter 39 at the end and Letter 40, note 38.
20. At the end of letter 17.

LETTER 46

Another copy of a letter written in response to our inquiries from myself to the same Successus.[1]

RUTH MAKES HERSELF plain to see for those who love her, but hides herself, I think, and tries to hide from the thoughts of intriguing men. They do not show themselves worthy to behold her with clear eyes. The lovers of blameless faith pray to the Lord "in integrity of heart"[2] as it is written, but those who walk in crooked paths and have "a crooked heart,"[3] according to the saying in the Psalms, gather for their own purposes intriguing pretexts of perverse designs in order to distort the straight ways of the Lord and lead astray the souls of those who are rather simple into the necessity of thinking what is not right. And I say this after having read the Memoranda from your holiness, and then found some things being proposed in them unsafely by those who have loved, I do not know how, the perversion of falsely named knowledge.

(2) And they were these: I. "If Emmanuel was composed of two natures, but after the union one incarnate nature of the Word is known, it will follow that it is by all means necessary to say that he suffered in his own nature."[4]

(3) The blessed Fathers who defined the august creed or

---

1. For the critical text of this letter see Schwartz, *ACO* 1.1.6 pp. 157–162. Geerard numbers this letter 5346 in *CPG*. See also Ebied-Wickham, *Unpublished Syriac Letters*, 39–43, and Wickham, *Select Letters*, 84–93. For another translation of this letter see M. Wiles and M. Santer, *Documents in Early Christian Thought* (New York, 1976), 66–71.
2. Wis 1.1.
3. Ps 100(101).4.
4. The Greek word is φύσις, here to be translated "nature," or the objection to Cyril's formula has no point.

profession of faith[5] said that he himself, the Word of God the Father, who is of his essence, the only begotten, through whom are all things, was made flesh and was incarnate, and, without doubt, we say that those holy men were not ignorant that the body united to the Word was animated by a rational soul. Therefore, if anyone says that the Word was made flesh, he confesses that the flesh which was united to him was not without a rational soul. Thus, as I think, or rather as it is, to speak boldly, the all-wise evangelist John said that "the Word was made flesh,"[6] not that he was united to flesh without a soul, far from it, nor that he endured a change or alteration, for he has remained what he was, that is, God by nature, and having taken to himself existence as man, that is, being born according to the flesh as we from a woman, again he remained the one Son, except that he is not fleshless as he was before, that is, before the period of the Incarnation when he clothed himself, so to speak, with our nature. But although the body united to him is not consubstantial to the Word begotten of God the Father, even though it is united with a rational soul, still our thought certainly presents to our mind the difference of the two natures which have been united, and yet we confess one Son, Christ and Lord, since the Word was made flesh. And whenever we say flesh, we are saying man.

(4) Accordingly what necessity is there that he suffered in his own nature,[7] if it should be said that after the union there is one incarnate *phusis* of the Word? For if there was not in the plans of the dispensation of the Incarnation that which had been begotten to endure the suffering, they would be speaking the truth, because if that which had been begotten to suffer did not exist, there would be in a way every necessity somehow that the suffering happen to the nature of the Word. But if in saying "made flesh," the entire plan of the dispensation with flesh is introduced, for he was made flesh in no other way except by "succoring the seed of Abraham"[8] and "in all things

5. At Nicaea.
6. Jn 1.14.

7. Cf. note 4.
8. Heb 2.16.

he was made like unto his brethren"[9] and by "taking the form of a slave,"[10] then in vain have they spoken nonsense who say that it follows that he must have endured suffering in his own nature, for his flesh is submitted to suffering, with regard to which reasonably the suffering would be considered to have occurred, since the Word is impassible. It is not for this reason that we exclude him from being said to have suffered. Just as the body became his own body, so also everything that is of the body with the exception of sin alone would be said to be no less his, since he made it his own according to the dispensation of his Incarnation.[11]

(5) But those on the opposite side will say: II. "If there was one incarnate nature of the Word,[12] in a way there is every necessity to say that a confusion and a blending occurred since the nature of man in him is lessened, as it were, and taken away."

(6) Again, those who "pervert what is right"[13] have not known that there is in truth one incarnate nature of the Word. For if there is one Son, who by nature and in truth is the Word of God the Father, the one ineffably begotten of him, who then according to an assumption of flesh, not without a soul but endowed with a rational soul, came forth a man from a woman, he shall not be for this reason divided into two persons and two sons but he has remained one, yet not without flesh nor outside his body, but having his own body according to an inseparable union. He who says this does not in any way or in any manner signify a confusion, or a blending, or anything else of such a kind, nor indeed will this follow as if from some necessary reasoning or other. For even if it is stated by us that the only-begotten Son of God is one, incarnate and made man, he is not mixed together because of this, as it seems to them. The nature of the Word has not passed over into the nature of the

9. Ibid., 17.
10. Phil 2.7.
11. In answering the objection Cyril expounds his beliefs, but does not seem to meet the point of it completely.
12. *Phusis*.
13. Mi 3.9.

flesh. Neither has the nature of the flesh passed over into the nature of the Word, but remaining and being considered in the propriety[14] according to the nature of each ineffably and inexplicably united, in accordance with the reasoning just given by us, this has shown forth for us the one *phusis*[15] of the Son; but, as I said, incarnate.

(7) For not only in the case of those which are simple by nature is the term 'one' truly used, but also in respect to what has been brought together according to a synthesis, as man is one being, who is of soul and body. For soul and body are of different species and are not consubstantial to each other, but when united they produce one *phusis* of man, even though in the considerations of the synthesis the difference exists according to the nature of those which have been brought together into a unity. Accordingly they are speaking in vain who say that, if there should be one incarnate *phusis* of the Word, in every way and in every manner it would follow that a mixture and a confusion occurred as if lessening and taking away the nature of man. For neither has it been lessened, nor is it taken away, as the question says. For to say that he has been made flesh is sufficient for the most complete statement of his becoming man. For if there had been silence about this on our part there would have been some room for their calumny. But since the statement that he was made flesh has been necessarily adduced, where is there a way of lessening or subtraction?

(8) And III. "If Christ is perfect God and if he is known to be perfect man, and if he is consubstantial to the Father according to divinity, but according to humanity consubstantial to us, where is the perfection if the nature of man no longer subsists? Where is the consubstantiality to us, if the essence, that is our nature, no longer subsists?"

(9) The solution or response in the previous section suffices as a clarification of these questions also. For if in saying "the one *phusis* of the Word" we had been silent by not mentioning

14. The Greek word is ἰδιότης, the Latin *proprietas*. Cf. Lampe, *PGL* 665, s.v., "ἰδιότης," and Wolfson, *Philosophy of the Fathers*, 1:408.
15. Cyril here uses his formula again.

"incarnate," but, as it were, setting aside the dispensation of his Incarnation, doubtless their statement would not have been incredible to them, as they pretend to ask, "where is the perfection in the humanity or how has the essence like to us subsisted?" But since the perfection of his humanity and the indication of an essence like unto us has been brought in by saying "incarnate," let them stop supporting themselves upon a rod made of reed. For whoever rejected the dispensation and denied the Incarnation, rightly was to be accused of robbing the Son of his perfect humanity. But if, as I said, in stating that he was made flesh there is a clear and unambiguous confession that he became man, nothing any longer hinders the meaning that, since he is the one and only Son and Christ, he is God and man and just as he is perfect in divinity so also is he in his humanity. And moreover your excellency very rightly and with complete understanding has expounded the matter concerning the Passion of our Savior, by strongly contending that the only-begotten Son of God in so far as he is known to be and is God did not endure the sufferings of the body in his own nature but suffered rather in his earthly nature.

(10) For it was necessary and proper to maintain with reference to the one true Son both that he did not suffer in his divinity and that it is affirmed that he suffered in his humanity, for his flesh suffered. But they again think that we are thereby introducing what is called by them *theopatheia*,[16] and they do not understand the dispensation, but most maliciously attempt to transfer the suffering to man separately, stupidly practicing a harmful reverence, so that the Word of God would not be confessed the Savior, as the one who gave his own blood for our sakes, but rather so that a man, considered separately and by himself, Jesus, might be said to set this aright. But thinking thus overthrows the entire plan of the dispensation with flesh and transforms our divine mystery with no uncertainty virtually into *anthrōpolatreia*,[17] and they do not understand that the

16. The Greek, Θεοπάθεια, signifies: "suffering on the part of God," or "God-suffering."

17. ᾿ανθρωπολατρεία, "the worship of a man."

blessed Paul said that the one who is of the Jews according to the flesh, that is, the Christ of the seed of Abraham and Jesse and David is, "the Lord of glory"[18] and "God blessed forever"[19] and "over all things," showing that the body of the Word is his own body, the one which was nailed to the wood, and attributing the cross to him through this.

(11) And IV. But I perceive that something else besides these matters is the thing being asked. For the one who says that the Lord suffered merely in his flesh is making the suffering irrational and involuntary. But if one would say that he suffered with his rational soul, in order that the suffering might be voluntary, nothing hinders one from saying that he suffered in the nature of his humanity. But if this is true, how will we not be granting that the two natures subsist indivisibly after the union? So that if one says "that Christ therefore suffered in his flesh"[20] for us, he is saying nothing else except that Christ therefore suffered for us in our nature.

(12) Again this question is no less in opposition to those who say that there is one incarnate *phusis* of the Word, and the proposers, desiring to prove that this formula is rather useless, eagerly strive to prove that two natures always subsisted. But they have ignored the fact that those things which are usually distinguished not just according to speculation, completely and specifically differ from one another in every manner separately into diversity. Let a man like unto us be an example for us again. For we know that there are two natures in him, one the nature of the soul and the other the nature of the body. But when we divide him merely in thought and conceive the difference in subtle speculations or the presentations of thought to the mind, we do not posit the natures one apart from the other, nor indeed do we at all impute to them virtual existence through the division, but we conceive of them as the natures of one man, so that the two no longer are two, but through them both the one living being is produced. Accord-

18. 1 Cor 2.8.
19. Rom 9.5.
20. Cf. 1 Pt 4.1.

ingly, even though they would speak of the nature of humanity and the nature of divinity in Emmanuel, still the humanity became the Word's own, and one Son is meant with his humanity.

(13) Since the divinely inspired Scripture says that he suffered in his flesh, it is better that we also speak thus, rather than to say in the nature of his humanity, even though, if this was not said by some perversely, in no way at all would they do injury to the statement of the mystery. For what else is the nature of his humanity except flesh animated rationally, in which flesh we say that the Lord has suffered? Hence they speak with undue precision of him suffering in the nature of the humanity, as if they separate it from the Word and set it apart by itself, so that they mean two and not one, the Word of God the Father still incarnate and made man. The word "indivisibly," added by them, seems somehow to us to be significant of true doctrine. But they do not think in this fashion, for the word "indivisible" with them is taken in a different sense according to the babblings of Nestorius. For they say that by equality of honor, by likeness of will, by authority is the man in whom he dwelled indivisible from the Word of God, so that they do not propose these words with simplicity but with some craftiness and malice.[21]

21. A textual problem occurs here. Migne (PG 77.245) notes that the last part of this letter is the same as the last part of Letter 40, and that Letter 46 ends here. Schwartz (*ACO* 1.1.6 pp. 157–162) does the same.

LETTER 47

From John, Bishop of Antioch, to Cyril, my fellow bishop, most beloved of God and most holy. Greetings.[1]

E HAVE WELCOMED one another back, my lord, with the blessing of God or by the intervention of my lord Paul the bishop, who is most God-fearing in all things to the benefit of us both and is a man careless of all things in his own regard provided that the causes of the disturbances in the churches of God might be lulled to rest and the greatest concord might exist for the glory of God. Hence he has returned in peace and all the personal observances of friendship toward your reverence have been fulfilled perfectly on our part, since besides the matters stated by your holiness in your reply we have consulted with each other on small points having no difference of meaning but involving administrative matters. I rather wish and pray that not only I myself but all of the most God-fearing lord bishops of the East join with your dear and honorable person, I mean your sincerity, which I consider of the greatest value. A short period separated us, and then again, with God willing it, we have returned to each other having soothed all causes of pain and having left nothing at all on either side worthy of strife or discord. This has not come to be without God, but with him as the source, and with the most Christ-loving and most God-fearing emperors using the authority proper to them.

(2) Let your reverence, therefore, receive Cassius and Amonius, my most pious subjects, not in order that they may be contentious with you, but so that what has been built up by you

1. For the critical text of this letter see Schwartz, *ACO* 1.1.7 p. 155. Geerard numbers this letter 5347 in *CPG*.

may be brought to stability and the fairest outcome. We recognize our gratitude to my lord, the most admirable and illustrious tribune and secretary, Aristolaus, who realized from the matters which were stirred up among us that it was better that we unite each other stalwartly and steadfastly by brief letters. Receive, therefore, I urge you, what we have composed well and with fair intent and with all the force needed to convince you, and have sent to you. Let no thought enter your mind that we have done anything unscrupulously in the matters proposed. Our conscience knows and invites God above as witness that we did not have unsound desires in your regard but desired to administer our own affairs for the benefit of the churches of Christ. The same most pious deacons will tell you the way we administered affairs. Everything has been completely done by us so that no one would be able to repudiate the agreement which has come to be. Receive, therefore, I urge you, in gladness the brethren who bring to you the benefits of peace and let your holiness pray that the matter proceed prosperously to the benefit of the churches of Christ.

(3) For just as we brought ourselves to you by the law of our disposition and entrusted ourselves to you so also we are anxious and desire or rather pray that no one of those with us may neglect to have the same opinions as we, since we are zealous with forbearance and with order in turn to draw along with us those of the least conviction or rather those who need guidance from us to the benefit of the Universal Church and her affairs.

(4) Accordingly realize fully that we ourselves are as you knew us to be previously, with the same disposition both when we send our letters to you and receive yours. For this will honor us and will be a crown for your holiness. We send most cordial greetings to the entire brotherhood with you.

LETTER 48

A letter of the same to Dynatus, Bishop of Ancient Nikopolis of Epirus.[1]

THOUGHT IT NECESSARY to set down for your reverence what is known to have followed hard upon the peace of the churches. Accordingly, there arrived at Antioch my lord, the most admirable tribune and secretary, Aristolaus, bearing imperial letters which advised the most pious Bishop of the Church of Antioch, John, to anathematize the abominable teachings of Nestorius, to approve his deposition in agreement with the holy council, and thus to seek communion with us. And this was the sense of the letters. Some of the bishops of the East, who had not yet condemned Nestorius, or who even were favoring his leadership, give offense to our true faith and in no slight way fight against the glory of Christ, the Savior of us all. They induced Acacius, the most God-fearing and most holy Bishop of Beroea, to write to me certain absurd things to the effect that, since they requested it, I ought to repudiate everything written by me against Nestorius and hurl them aside as no longer in force, and agree only to the profession of faith defined by the holy Fathers in the city of Nicaea. And your holiness knows that such were their conditions before in the city of Ephesus. But I wrote in answer to these matters that they were requesting something not acceptable, for we have properly written what we have written in accordance with the true and blameless faith and we deny none at all of our own writings. Not a thing was said, as they stated,

1. For the critical text of this letter see Schwartz, *ACO* 1.1.4 pp. 31–32. Geerard numbers this letter 5348 in *CPG*. See also Festugière, *Éphèse*, 505–507.

carelessly, but what I said was entirely and in every way necessary and concurrent with the meaning of the truth. Rather it was proper that they should not have made use of such detours and delays and should not carry it beyond what was necessary. They should acquiesce in the decisions of the most God-fearing and most God-loving emperor himself, anathematize the nonsense of Nestorius and the blasphemies which existed against Christ, approve his deposition, and agree to the consecration of the most holy and most God-fearing bishop, Maximian.

(2) After they had all seen from these letters sent by me to them that they would not receive communion with us unless those things which they ought to do were carried to completion, they send to Alexandria the most pious and most God-loving Bishop of Emesa, Paul, who bore letters to me concerning communion but not very properly composed. For they pretended to bring forward reproofs as if some things were not properly said and done in the holy synod. I did not accept such letters but I maintained how they only could add second insults, who were in need of forgiveness for their previous ones.

(3) When the most God-fearing bishop already mentioned apologized and strongly maintained under oath that he had not had such an intention, but rather had come to the letter in a spirit of simplicity, I accepted this through charity. But I did not agree to be united with him unless by having given me a written document he anathematized the teachings of Nestorius and agreed that he had been deposed and assented to the consecration of the most pious bishop, Maximian. And he asked that by having received such documents in behalf of all the most God-fearing bishops of the East we would demand nothing more from them. I objected in no way, but I sent along with my lord, the most admirable tribune and secretary, Aristolaus, two of our clerics to Antioch after placing a document in their hands and saying that if the most God-fearing Bishop of Antioch, John, would sign it and accept it, then let them give him the letters of communion. For the most admirable tribune, Aristolaus, already mentioned, objected to the delay.

(4) Accordingly when the most God-fearing bishop, John, and the illustrious bishops with him signed it, and after they anathematized the teachings of Nestorius and agreed that he had been deposed and assented to the consecration of the most pious and the most God-fearing bishop, Maximian, we have granted them communion. For this was offered to them by the holy council at the capital city of Ephesus.

(5) And let your holiness know this also, that the most pious and God-fearing bishop, Paul, began exhorting me very much at first in behalf of those deposed, namely, Palladius, Eutherius, Himerius and Dorotheus,[2] and asked that the decisions against them be abrogated, stoutly maintaining that otherwise the peace of the churches was not able to be carried to completion unless this also was offered. But I said that he was putting his hand to an impossible task, and that this would never be an offer on our part. Accordingly they have remained in the schism in which they still are now and no mention of them was made in the agreements concerning the peace of the holy churches.

(6) The others[3] have written the letter which they sent to me and to the most God-fearing and most holy bishops, namely, both Sixtus, Bishop of the Church of the great city of Rome and Maximian, Bishop of the holy Church of Constantinople. And it was necessary that your excellency be clearly informed of these matters, lest some, who are accustomed to trifle in one thing or another, might upset some of the brethren by saying that we retracted what we have written against the blasphemies of Nestorius. I also sent to you copies of my letters, that is, of the one written by me to John, the most pious Bishop of Antioch, and of the one written by him to me about anathematizing the blasphemies of Nestorius and about his deposition, so that your excellency might clearly understand. And let no one deliver to you any other letters concerning these matters.

(7) Salute the brotherhood with you. The brethren with us salute you in the Lord.

2. Cf. Letter 11, note 3 and Letter 90.
3. John of Antioch and his fellow bishops. See Letter 35.

LETTER 49

To my lord, beloved brother and archbishop, Maximian, Cyril sends greetings in the Lord.[1]

HERE WAS NO DOUBT that the prayers of your holiness were always and in every way efficacious. The Savior of us all readily nods assent to those who love him so that each with joy and exultation at this says, "From his holy temple he heard my voice, and my cry to him will reach his ears."[2] Behold, behold the limbs of the body of the church which had been torn apart have been joined again to each other and nothing severs into discord those ministering the Gospel of Christ. We all are crowned in one faith since we have driven out of the sacred enclosures Nestorius, the inventor of impieties, and have removed from the noble flock a false shepherd. This one success has come to be as a result of your prayers.

(2) Since, therefore, peace concerning the churches became a necessary anxiety for the most pious emperors, we ourselves are also praying that there may disappear from our midst the wall dividing us and severing us unto discord. We pray that the peace which is most pleasing to God may blaze up like light, since John, the most God-loving and most God-fearing Bishop of the Church of Antioch, and the most pious bishops with him have agreed in writing that they hold Nestorius deposed, and that they anathematize his unholy blasphemies. I have sent letters of communion to his reverence and to the other bishops. We have joined in unanimity since your holiness and

---

1. For the critical text of this letter see Schwartz, *ACO* 1.1.4 p. 34. Geerard numbers this letter 5349 in *CPG*. See also Festugière, *Éphèse*, 510–511.
2. Ps 17.7.

all the other bishops, who constituted the entirety of the holy council, concur in this. Strife and discord do not prevail with us. We all have had the one intention, which looks toward peace. If indeed they who in the beginning disagreed with us and severed themselves from us had desired it, there would not have been any strife and separation among the churches at all.

(3) May our Savior be blessed, who brought the storm to an end, and spread abroad the calm of peace because of the prayers and intercession of your holiness and of all others who because they have the true and sincere faith render to him adoration and service in the Spirit and in truth.

LETTER 50

To my beloved lord and fellow bishop Valerian, Bishop of Iconium, Cyril sends greetings in the Lord.[1]

T IS SUFFICIENT, as I see it, or rather it is the nature of truth, to invoke the prudence of your holiness[2] very manfully and as far as possible to place accuracy in opposition to the random remarks of some people. Like old gossips they use frigid phrases mixing everything up and down and pretending to be subtly busy concerning the mystery of the Incarnation of the Lord, the only begotten. Yet they do not even perceive this, but change the mystery to what is not right, and do this contentedly, while they hold perverted doctrines. In these matters the most difficult thing is this, that they pretend to want to have upright ideas and by pretending to have the appearance of an inclination toward this, as if they had fitted on a mask, they pour the poison of the impiety of Nestorius into the souls of simpler men. In a way they are like unto the healers of human bodies, that is, the doctors who stir sweet honey with their bitter medicines. Beguiling by the quality of what is useful they remove the perception of what is naturally disagreeable.

(2) But we are not ignorant of their ideas, since "we have the mind of Christ,"[3] according to the most learned Paul. If there was someone who said that God the only begotten Word, who was ineffably begotten of God the Father, and is the creator of the very ages, had a beginning of his existence from the Holy

---

1. For the critical text of this letter see Schwartz, *ACO* 1.1.3 pp. 90–101. Geerard numbers this letter 5350 in *CPG*. See also Festugière, *Éphèse*, 453–466.
2. Bishop of Iconium in Lycaonia, Asia Minor.
3. 1 Cor 2.16.

Virgin, to them he would not seem to have missed the mark in what he said. If the Word of God by nature is spirit, how was he begotten from flesh, for the Lord says, "That which is born of the flesh is flesh?"[4] Since the doctrine concerning the mystery of Christ treads another path or road toward what is direct and fixed and has no distortion, why do they babble in vain, "when they understand neither what they say nor the things about which they make assertion?"[5]

(3) We say that the only begotten Word of God, being spirit as God, according to the Scriptures,[6] for the salvation of men was made flesh and became man, not by transmuting a body for himself from his own nature, nor by being deprived of being what he was, nor by having sustained a change or alteration, but by taking his undefiled body from the Holy Virgin, a body animated rationally. Thus he proved that body to be his own in an incomprehensible, unconfused and entirely ineffable union, not as the body of someone else but known as his very own. Thus the only begotten came into the world as "the firstborn,"[7] and the one not to be classed with creation was, insofar as he is known to be God, "among many brethren." Accordingly when it is said that he was born, and "of a woman,"[8] necessarily it is also inferred that he was born according to the flesh, in order that he might not be considered as taking a beginning of his existence from the Holy Virgin. Although he existed before all ages and is God the Word coeternal and subsists in a unity with his own Father, yet when he desired to "take the form of a slave"[9] according to the goodwill of his Father, then it is said he submitted to birth from a woman according to the flesh like unto us. Therefore, admittedly what is begotten from the flesh is flesh, but what is begotten of God is God. But Christ is both by himself, being one Son and Lord with his own flesh yet not inanimate, as I said, but animated rationally.

---

4. Jn 3.6. This part of the sentence and the quotation express the ideas of Cyril's opponents.

5. 1 Tm 1.7.
6. Cf. Jn 4.24.
7. Rom 8.29.

8. Gal 4.4.
9. Phil 2.7.

(4) Let them, therefore, not divide for us the one Son, setting the Word separate and one Son apart, and separate from him setting the man from a woman, as they say, but let them rather know that God the Word was not connected to a man, but it is stated that he became man "succoring the offspring of Abraham,"[10] according to the Scriptures, and having been "made like unto his brethren"[11] in all things, sin alone excepted.[12] This likeness in every way he would properly have and, above all other similarities, his birth from a woman, which in us is considered proper to human nature and is like us, but in the only begotten it is perceived as going beyond this, for God was made flesh. Accordingly the Holy Virgin is called *Theotokos*.[13]

(5) If they should say that God and man by coming together in one constituted the one Christ with the *hupostasis* of each obviously preserved unblended but distinguished by reason, it is possible to see that they are thinking and saying nothing accurate in this. God and man by coming together did not constitute the one Christ, as they say, but, as I said, the Word being already God partook of blood and flesh like unto us in order that God would be known to have been made man and to have taken our flesh and to have made it his own, in order that, just as a man such as we are is known to be one, composed of soul and body, so also he is confessed to be one, both Son and Lord.

(6) The nature of man is admitted to be one, and to be one *hupostasis*, even if it is known to be of different realities of diverse kinds. For the body admittedly is of a different nature relative to the soul, but it is the soul's own body, and helps to complete the *hupostasis* of the one man. Although in our mind and our thinking the difference between the soul and body mentioned is not obscure, yet their coming together or meeting, since it is undivided, constitutes one living man. Hence the only begotten Word of God did not come forth as man by assuming a man, but, although he had an ineffable begetting

10. Heb 2.17.
11. Ibid.

12. Cf. Heb 4.15 and 2 Cor 5.21.
13. Mother of God.

from God the Father, he became man by having fashioned for himself a temple through the holy and consubstantial Spirit. Wherefore also he is known to be one, even though in thought according to our reasoning his body was of a different nature relative to him. And let it be confessed in every way that his body was not inanimate, but was animated by a rational soul.

(7) I have learned that some have come to such a point of madness as not to shrink from saying that God the Word, by indwelling in a certain Son born of the Virgin, deified him. But, my good men, I would say to them, this is not the Word of God made flesh and made man, but rather the dwelling in a man just as, of course, in one of the holy prophets! But the account of the mystery in relation to us, as was clarified in the statements just made above, means that "the Word" begotten of God the Father "was made flesh"[14] according to the Scriptures. Not that he endured an alteration of nature, or variation, or change, I mean into flesh, but that he made flesh his own, flesh rationally animated, and he came forth a man. He was not joined to or dwelling in a man, as they say. To say that the one who has had the indwelling has been deified, as they maintain (for this is completely to be cast aside in our estimation), how does this not have every indication of sheer stupidity? It is in opposition to the scope of Sacred Scripture.

(8) The divinely inspired Paul says that the Word of God, though he was by nature God and equal in all things whatsoever to his Father, "did not consider being equal to God a thing to be clung to, but emptied himself," and "took the form of a slave" and "was made like men" "as man" and "humbled himself."[15] But they, by changing the nature of things to the totally opposite, and impiously huckstering off the meaning of the truth, say that a man has been deified. Then, my good men, who is the one who emptied himself and how has he humbled himself? Tell me, what kind of form of a slave did he take? For their reasoning, as it seems to us, introduces a man lifted up from being humble like unto us, who ascends from emptiness

14. Jn 1.14.
15. Phil 2.6–8.

like unto us to the fullness of the divinity, and who is changed
from the form of a slave to that of the master. How, therefore,
they say that the only begotten emptied himself, or how he
endured our humility, I am not able to understand, unless they
are saying that he has emptied himself because he has honored
man with his own glory. If, by honoring man, he is wronged; if,
by glorifying man, he is emptied; how will one not say better
that he granted neither honor nor glory to anyone? He would
remain in his own preeminence, if he neither honored nor
glorified the man who, as they say, was appropriated by him.

(9) Do not the things which they determined to think and
delight to say seem worthy in every way somehow of laughter
and full of extreme stupidity? But the statement of the truth
would not raise any suspicion that he was ever emptied, if he
did not have fullness according to his own nature, neither
would there be a thought that he humbled himself, if he was
not utterly sublime and most high in position and then descended unto what he was not. He who takes the form of a slave
will know completely without doubt that he has freedom by
nature before he takes the form of a slave, and he who became
man did not know that he was this before he has become man.

(10) Since, therefore, the holy and divinely inspired Scripture names this an emptying and the form of a slave and
moreover also the humanity, and says that the one who freely
endured these is the Word of God the Father, why do they
pervert to the opposite meaning the wisdom of the well-
devised dispensation, and say that a man has been deified, with
the purpose in mind that Christians still are no different from
those who have "served the creature rather than the creator"?[16]
Perhaps they will somehow concede that the holy angels themselves have been led into error along with us. The Sacred
Scripture says that the angels had been enjoined to adore the
firstborn when he was brought into the world.[17] How would
they apply the name firstborn to the only begotten unless he
was incarnate? For if the saying is true, "firstborn among many

16. Rom 1.25.
17. Cf. Heb 1.6.

brethren"[18] then rightly is he known to be the firstborn, since he descended unto brotherhood, which is obviously brotherhood with us, since he became man as we are, having been made like his brethren in all things,[19] sin alone excepted.[20] This consideration and thought would be enough for our piety that the flesh of God, the begetter of life in regard to everything, having come into being, has his life-giving power and force, and it enriches his unspeakable and unapproachable glory.

(11) But it is likely that they who have determined to hold these ideas add other slanders against the holy teachings, which slanders take away from the person[21] of the only begotten the insults which he endured at the hands of the Jews and, in addition to these, the very death according to the flesh, and assign them as if to another separate son of a woman. For it seems best to them, I do not know how, by the path not directed to piety to leap into the trap of Hades and the pit of Hell[22] according to the Scripture. Admittedly the divine, because it is without a body, is untouchable and entirely intact, because the divine is beyond every creature, both visible and intelligible, and in nature incorporeal, immaculate, untouchable and incomprehensible. Since the only begotten Word of God, having taken a body from the Holy Virgin, and, as I already said over and over again, having made it his own offered himself in an odor of sweetness[23] to God the Father as a spotless sacrifice, in this way it is asserted that he endured on our behalf what happened to his flesh. Everything that happened to flesh would rightly be attributed to him, sin alone excepted, for it is his own body. Accordingly since God the Word became man, he remained impassible as God, but, because he necessarily made the things of his flesh his own, it is asserted that he endured what is according to flesh, although he is without experience of suffering in so far as he is thought of as God.

(12) Therefore, an appearance of piety leads them away

---

18. Rom 8.29.   21. πρόσωπον, in Greek.
19. Cf. Heb 2.17.   22. Prv 9.18.
20. Cf. Heb 4.15 and 2 Cor 5.21.
23. Cf. Ex 29.18, Ez 20.41, and Eph 5.2.

from the truth, because they do not perceive that his impassibility has been preserved insofar as he has divine existence and is God, but the suffering for us according to his flesh is also attributed to him insofar as, being God by nature, he became flesh, that is a complete man. For who was he who said to God the Father in heaven, "Sacrifice and oblation you would not, but a body you have fitted to me. [In holocausts and sin-offerings you have had no pleasure.] Then said I, 'Behold, I come to do your will, O God.'"[24] For he who as God was without a body says that the body was fitted to him so that, when he offered this for us, he might cure us all "by his stripes"[25] according to the saying of the prophet. But how is it that "one died for all,"[26] one who is worth all others, if the suffering is considered simply that of some man? If he suffered according to his human nature, since he made the sufferings of his body his own, then, indeed, we say, and very rightly, that the death of him alone according to the flesh is known to be worth the life of all, not the death of one who is as we are, even though he became like unto us, but we say that he, being God by nature, became flesh and was made man according to the confession of the Fathers.

(13) But if some take away from the only begotten the suffering according to flesh as ugly and incongruous and improper, let them for the same reasons take away from him also his birth according to the flesh from the Holy Virgin. For if the statement that he suffered in his flesh is improper to him, how is not that which came before the suffering, that is, his birth according to flesh or even, to speak out once and for all, the manner of his becoming man? Thus the Christian mystery is gone, and the hope of salvation is henceforward rendered meaningless.

(14) "But how," someone says, "would he suffer who did not know suffering?" The Word of God, as I said, is admittedly impassible in his own nature, but it is stated that he suffered in his own flesh, according to the Scriptures, for he himself was in

24. Cf. Heb 10.5–7, Ps 39(40).7–9.
25. Is 53.5.
26. 2 Cor 5.14.

his suffering body. And Peter will give you proof since he writes about him, "who himself bore our sins in his body upon the tree."[27] Therefore, the Word is impassible when he is considered God by nature, yet the sufferings of his flesh are known to be his according to the economy of the dispensation. For in what way would he who is "the firstborn of every creature"[28] through whom have come to be principalities and powers, thrones and dominations,[29] in whom all things hold together, have become "the firstborn of the dead,"[30] and "the first-fruits of those who have fallen asleep,"[31] unless the Word, being God, made his own the body born to suffer? But just as he was "born from a woman"[32] according to the flesh and made his own a birth like unto us in his human nature, although he has his own begetting from his Father, so also it is stated that he suffered in his flesh and in his human nature like unto us, although impassibility was his by nature in so far as he is considered God. Thus is he known to be Christ, thus is he also seated with his Father, not as a man honored by the indwelling of God the Word, but as the Son in truth even when he became man. For the dignity of his essential, preeminent excellence is preserved for him, even if he has appeared in "the form of a slave"[33] according to the dispensation. Therefore, as I say, even if he was partaker of our nature as man, still he was at the same time above all creation as God.

(15) But I learned of someone explaining the cause of the Ascension into the heavens who said that he ascended to a safe and secure place and was deemed worthy of sitting together with the Father, and there, he said, the enemy of our nature is not able to plot against him again and approach him. Tell me, then, has heaven become a citadel for him and has his departure from us, about which we even exult, become a flight, not an ascension? But he feared, so it seems, that the evil one would construct a second snare for him in some way, I suppose, and if he had not ascended, there would be snares laid for him, as it

27. 1 Pt 2.24.
28. Col 1.15.
29. Cf. Col 1.16.
30. Cf. ibid., 18.

31. 1 Cor 15.20.
32. Gal 4.4.
33. Phil 2.7.

appears, even after the Resurrection. Who will not depart far from such vomitings, or who will not rise and go away from talk of marvels so disgraceful, bidding a long farewell to those daring to think or say such things? Away with thought so exceedingly loathsome and fallen! I think that nothing is more senile or more stupid. The matter has reached such a point of vulgarity of thoughts on their part that nothing is more disgraceful. When Christ had completed the dispensation with us, trampled on satan, thrown down all his power and destroyed "the power of death"[34] itself, he restored for us a new and living way by having ascended "into heaven" and having "appeared before the face of God the Father on our behalf,"[35] as it is written. He is seated with him even in flesh, not as a man considered separately and a different son besides the Word, nor as a man having him indwelling, but as the Son being truly the one and only Son even when he became man. Accordingly he is seated with him as God with God, and Lord with Lord, and as Son with his Father in truth, being this by nature even though he is known to be with flesh.

(16) And perhaps it would not be difficult by still longer discussions to point out the depth of their ignorance, but refuting such vain ideas of theirs by still more arguments is somehow perhaps being stupid at the same level as those babbling those trifles. I think it is no doubt necessary, in addition to what has been said, to attack the means by which they think they are able to frighten the congregation of the Lord, as it is written and "to shoot in the dark at the upright of heart,"[36] that is, those who have chosen to pass their lives in simplicity of purpose and who have received into their souls the tradition of faith as a certain trust and keep it holy and free from harm. Those who are clever at deceit and, by the intricately woven novelties of their thoughts, carry as quarry the less learned away from faith in the truth, by imitating the wickedness of the rest of heretics ignorantly offer what is usual with heretics

34. Cf. Heb 2.14.
35. Heb 9.24.
36. Ps 10(11).2.

without considering what is written, "Woe to him giving his neighbor foul subversion to drink."[37]

(17) Those who shield the impiety of Arius say that the only begotten Word of God is of a different essence. They place him second to the one who begot him and stoutly maintain that he is a creature and begotten, and place among creation him "through whom are all things"[38] and "in whom are all things."[39] Then, meddling in the mystery of the only begotten's dispensation with flesh, most mischievously they corrupt the force of the truth and also are subject to charges of the opinion of Apollinaris for they confidently affirm that the Word of God took flesh, but flesh in no way animated rationally. Rather they say that he was in place of mind and soul in the body. But, as I said, in doing this they are caught most villainously. In order that we may not think that the human statements of our Lord were made according to the dispensation and according to the measure proper to the humanity since he became man, they defraud his flesh of the rational soul indwelling in it. Thus they drag him down and say that he is essentially among those less than the Father and collect pretexts of their calumny against him from the Holy Scriptures.

(18) But see, even now the emulators of their ignorance rise up bitterly against those who do not admit the "empty prattlings"[40] of Nestorius, and besiege the true and blameless faith after gathering together the garbage of their worthless ideas. For they say that the divinely inspired Paul states concerning Christ the Savior of us all, that "He emptied himself, taking the form of a slave and being made like unto men and being found in form as a man he humbled himself, becoming obedient to death, even to death on a cross. Therefore God also has exalted him and has bestowed upon him the name that is above every name."[41] And indeed somewhere else he says that, "God was in Christ reconciling the world to himself"[42] and again, "in whom dwells all the fullness of the Godhead bodily."[43] And they

---

37. Cf. Hb 2.15.
38. Rom 11.36.
39. Col 1.16.
40. 1 Tim 6.20.

41. Phil 2.6–9.
42. 2 Cor 5.19.
43. Col 2.9.

accommodate themselves to the words of Peter since he once said, "how God anointed Jesus of Nazareth with the Holy Spirit and with power, and he went about doing good and healing all who were in the power of the devil; for God was with him,"[44] and again, "The times of this ignorance God has, it is true, overlooked, but now he calls upon all men everywhere to repent; inasmuch as he has fixed a day of judgment on which he will judge the world with justice by a man whom he has appointed, and whom he has guaranteed to all by raising him from the dead."[45]

(19) By proposing these words and those stated in another way according to his humanity and by fashioning sharp arguments from their wretched considerations they at once ask, to whom has God the Father given the name above every name? To his own Word? And how is that not simply an incredible thing, they say. For he was always God begotten of him according to nature. This name would rightly be considered the name above every name. For what name is beyond that of God by nature? And whom did he anoint with the Holy Spirit or with whom was God? And bringing in other subjects besides, they jumble matters exceedingly and fill the minds of rather guileless men with uproar.

(20) Making distinctions in every direction, for they are "sensual men, not having the Spirit,"[46] and dividing the one Christ and Son and Lord into two sons, they will be caught as a result of their own undertakings. For they pretend to confess one Christ and Son and say that his person is one, but dividing him again into two *hupostaseis* separated and disjoined from one another they completely sweep away the doctrine of the mystery. They do indeed say that the one from a woman, that is, the form of a slave, separately and by himself received the name above every name, underwent the anointing of the Holy Spirit and the continual abiding possession of God, that is, the Word of God the Father. But they manifestly are belching up

44. Acts 10.38.
45. Acts 17.30, 31.
46. Jude 19.

arguments that smell foully of fatuity the most extreme of all. For "being evil" they would not be able "to speak good things"[47] according to the saying of the Savior.

(21) Confessedly he was and is always God and Lord who has his invisible and ineffable begetting from God the Father. Because he was born of a woman according to flesh in a marvelous manner and beyond us in the visitation of the Holy Spirit upon her and the overshadowing of the power of God,[48] and because he endured a birth like unto us, for thus we state he emptied himself and humbled himself and became obedient to death and the cross,[49] in this way and very rightly it is stated that he received the name that is above every name, so that "every knee bends to him of those in heaven, on earth and under the earth, and every tongue will confess that the Lord Jesus Christ is in the glory of God the Father."[50]

(22) For no reasonable creature was ignorant that the Word who became man was God. For even if he came to be like unto us and shared in like manner in blood and flesh,[51] still he did not therefore abandon being God nor did it make him cast aside being what he was, for he remained adorable in the glory of God the Father. His glory is to have his own Son ruling with him and being adored with him even though according to the dispensation he became man in order that he might save all creation under heaven.

(23) Therefore, when it was believed on the part of the holy angels and on our part who are on the earth that even in flesh he is God by nature and in truth, then he is known to have received the name above every name. Not that he profited in the matter by way of an addition, for he who was and always is, how could he receive as one not having, but rather because God the Father illuminated the minds of all and has not allowed it to be unknown that the incarnate Word is God by nature, for he says, "No one can come to me unless the Father who sent me draws him."[52]

47. Mt 12.34.
48. Cf. Lk 1.35.
49. Cf. Phil 2.6–9.

50. Cf. Phil 2.9–11.
51. Heb 2.14.
52. Jn 6.44.

(24) And his anointing also was with regard to his humanity. Since the only begotten Son, who is begotten of the Father, is holy according to nature just as is the Father, it is said that he was anointed as man, that is, sanctified by the Father insofar as he was manifestly a man. Hence the all-wise Paul writes about him and about us, "For both he who sanctifies and they who are sanctified are all from one. For which cause he is not ashamed to call them brethren, saying, 'I will declare thy name to my brethren.'"[53] Therefore when the only begotten, being holy according to nature and sanctifying creation, bore the title of our brother, then we state that he was anointed as a man among us not despising the measure[54] proper and fitting to his humanity because of the dispensation. For thus he speaks to the divinely inspired Baptist, "It becomes us to fulfill all justice."[55]

(25) But if God might be said to be with him, how did those acute sophists not know that the Father is always by nature with the Son being in him and having him with him? Or have they not recalled Christ saying, "Have I been so long a time with you, and you have not known me, Philip? He who has seen me, has seen the Father."[56] "I and the Father are one."[57] "Do you not believe that I am in the Father and the Father in me?"[58] But he also spoke elsewhere to his disciples saying, "The hour is coming and has arrived for you to be scattered, each one to his own house, and to leave me alone. But I am not alone, because the Father is with me."[59] Not as they think, who are stupidly filled with the vomitings of others, that the Word being God was as if he were one Son being with another son, the man assumed. This is a cutting and a division introducing a duality of sons. But God the Father was with the Son, that is, with the Word of God made flesh and made man, for the Father is inseparable from the Son.

(26) And even if God "will judge the world by a man whom he has appointed,"[60] no one in his right mind would think that

53. Heb 2.11, 12.
54. Cf. Eph 4.13.
55. Mt 3.15.
56. Jn 14.9.

57. Jn 10.30.
58. Jn 14.10.
59. Jn 16.32.
60. Acts 17.31.

Holy Scripture says that the only begotten, as if he was in a man considered separate from the Son born of a woman, will judge all under heaven. But we stoutly maintain rather that, of necessity, this is the holy thing to think, the very thing which Christ says, "For neither does the Father judge any man, but all judgment he has given to the Son, that all men may honor the Son even as they honor the Father."[61] For God the Word, although made man[62] and classed among men and named man in common with us, nevertheless, will be judge as God and Lord and the one Son,[63] since God the Father is in him then also.[64] For he has, as I said, the Father in him and he is in the Father. Just as there is one God the Father from whom are all things, so there is one Lord Jesus Christ through whom are all things.

(27) They, nevertheless, distort into something ugly even what was rightly said through the voice of the blessed Paul. For he said, and very correctly, "God was truly in Christ, reconciling the world to himself."[65] But they by again introducing a certain coarse incision in the one Christ and Son totally tear apart God the Word and say that he is in some other Christ considered apart, in order that he may be considered to have had an indwelling in a man rather than to have become incarnate. But, O wise men, the scope of Holy Scripture does not permit these to be true. You have confused the reading and the meaning of the ideas by turning them aside to what is improper. Yet it is necessary for us to "bring every mind into captivity to the obedience of Christ"[66] as it is written. For God was in him reconciling the world in Christ. When we are reconciled to Christ, we effect reconciliation with God the Father, since God the Word, who is begotten of him, is not different from him as far as identity of essence is considered, injuring himself in no way, even if he became man, as far as his being the one Son by nature is concerned. He was this even after he became flesh. That we have a reconciliation in Christ

---

61. Jn 5.22, 23.
62. Cf. Jn 1.14.
63. 1 Cor 8.6.

64. Cf. Jn 14.11.
65. 2 Cor 5.19.
66. Ibid. 10.5.

and that "he is our peace"[67] who dares to deny? For he is "the door"[68] and "the way"[69] and "in him dwells all the fullness of the Godhead bodily."[70]

(28) But again the one who is sharp in theory and clever at calumny lifts his ear upright and says, "if he who indwells is one, and likewise he is another in whom he is said to dwell, how is it not necessary to divide the *hupostaseis* and to say that each one subsists apart, and then tell me, where at length is there one person[71] left?" For if they pretend to say there is one person of Christ, while there are two *hupostaseis* separate and distinct, by all means there will be two persons also. But they come in like legislators confirming in all ways and in every manner what seems to them as being right. For they say, while separating the *hupostaseis*, we unite the person.

(29) But how is this not incredible and ignorant and impossible? By speculation one would perceive, as I said, that the flesh is of different essence from the Word united to it. But since the divinely inspired Scriptures say that there is one Son and Christ and Lord and the tradition of the faith has it so and not otherwise, we, by asserting the indissoluble union of the Word of God the Father with flesh, rationally animated, confess that there is one Christ and Son. And since there is one Son, we say that his is one person following in every way the divine and holy Gospel and those who were from the beginning eyewitnesses and servants of the Word. But we dismiss from communion with us those who have been accustomed to think something different from this and have turned themselves aside to what they should not by the inventions of inept syllogisms, saying to them, "Walk by the light of your own fire and by the flares you have burnt."[72]

(30) But since I have learned that some of these foolish men go about saying that the perverse teaching of Nestorius has prevailed among all the most God-fearing bishops in the East and is considered to be right by them and that it is necessary to follow it, I thought that the following ought to be made clear,

67. Eph 2.14.
68. Jn 10.7.
69. Ibid. 14.6.

70. Col 2.9.
71. πρόσωπον, in Greek. See note 21.
72. Is 50.11.

for the most God-fearing bishops throughout all the East along with my lord John, the most God-fearing Bishop of the Church of Antioch, made it clear to all through a written and clear confession that they condemn the "profane novelties"[73] of Nestorius and anathematize them with us and they never thought them worthy of any consideration but follow the evangelic and apostolic doctrines and harm in no manner the confession of the Fathers.

(31) For they also confessed with us that the Holy Virgin is the Mother of God[74] and did not add that she is the Mother of Christ[75] or the Mother of a man,[76] as those say who defend the unhappy and loathed opinions of Nestorius. But they said distinctly that there is one Christ and Son and Lord, God the Word ineffably begotten of God the Father before all ages and that he was begotten in most recent times of a woman according to flesh, so that he is both God and man at once, perfect in divinity and perfect in humanity. And they believe that his person[77] is one separating him in no way into two sons, or christs, or lords. If some men telling lies, therefore, say that the bishops of the East think anything different from these statements, let them not be believed, but let them be sent away as cheats and liars down to their father the devil so that they may not upset those who desire to walk uprightly. If some men fabricate letters for their own purposes and bring them around as if they were written by the person of more illustrious men than they, they ought not to be believed. How are those who once confessed the faith in writing able to write something else, as if they were carried away by repentance to the state of not wishing to think the truth.

(32) Salute the brotherhood with you. The brethren with us salute you in the Lord. I pray that you are well in the Lord.

73. 1 Tm 6.20.

74. Θεοτόκος.

75. χριστοτόκος.

76. ᾽ανθρωποτόκος.

77. πρόσωπον, see note 71.

GENERAL INDEX

Numbers refer to letter and paragraph

INDEX OF HOLY SCRIPTURE

(Books of the Old Testament)
Numbers refer to letter and paragraph.

(Books of the New Testament)